Real Artists Don't Starve

Timeless Strategies for Thriving in the New Creative Age

JEFF GOINS

Bestselling Author of *The Art of Work*

D0048895

Praise for *Real Artists Don't Starve*

"Jeff Goins doesn't just show us how to be more creative. He also reveals a path for turning our art into business and our business into art. Every entrepreneur, writer, and artist should read this book and take notes."

—DANIEL H. PINK, AUTHOR OF *DRIVE* AND *TO SELL IS HUMAN*

"Jeff Goins is back with his most powerful book yet. Every page offers insight, hope, and practical advice for anyone who wants to make their dent in the universe."

—SETH GODIN, AUTHOR OF *LINCHPIN*

"Jeff Goins has established himself as a fresh and dynamic voice inspiring us to get out of our own way and produce our best work. *Real Artists Don't Starve* is the work of angels: a book every aspiring writer, artist, and creative must read."

—STEVEN PRESSFIELD, BESTSELLING AUTHOR OF *THE WAR OF ART*

"I absolutely love that Jeff makes such a compelling case that being an artist isn't an either/or decision when it comes to money. It's not 'be a real artist and starve' or 'make money and quit being an artist.' Best of all, this book is perfectly timed for a digital world where we all have the opportunity to apply the principles in this book and create real art for real money!"

—JON ACUFF, *NEW YORK TIMES* BESTSELLING AUTHOR

"Anyone trying to make a living from their creative work will find much to steal here."

—AUSTIN KLEON, AUTHOR OF *STEAL LIKE AN ARTIST*

"Jeff puts to rest the myth of the starving artist. Artists not only deserve to be well rewarded, but there are more opportunities than ever for them to make it happen. This book is not only the blueprint, it's also Jeff's personal artistic manifesto. And now it's mine."

—JAMES ALTUCHER, AUTHOR AND ENTREPRENEUR

"In a world where work is increasingly commoditized and automated, creativity should command a greater premium than ever before . . . but it doesn't. Artists of all kinds seldom realize their own unique value, and their careers and creations suffer as a result. *Real Artists Don't Starve* unleashes the potential of artists and builds upon Jeff Goins's passion for empowering artists that enrich life as we know it."

—SCOTT BELSKY, ENTREPRENEUR, INVESTOR, AND
AUTHOR OF *MAKING IDEAS HAPPEN*

"It's one thing to want to be more creative. It's another to learn the art of doing creative work. In this book, my friend Jeff Goins shows us how to take our creative talents and turn them into a full-time living. Don't miss this!"

—JEREMY COWART, PHOTOGRAPHER AND
FOUNDER OF THE PURPOSE HOTEL

"Goins dispels the myth that being a creative is some illusive, mysterious dimension reserved for a chosen few. Instead, he reminds us that being an artist is a job that any motivated person can do with a strategic focus on inspiration-gathering, collaboration, risk-taking, discipline, and marketing. A great book for anyone bogged down by old-fashioned ideas about what it takes to be a thriving artist."

—LISA CONGDON, ARTIST AND AUTHOR OF *ART INC: THE
ESSENTIAL GUIDE TO BUILDING YOUR CAREER AS AN ARTIST*

"*Real Artists Don't Starve* provides practical, roll-up-your-sleeves approaches to succeeding creatively and financially as an artist. It's a treasure trove. I loved it!"

—KEVIN GRIFFIN, PLATINUM-SELLING SONGWRITER AND MEMBER OF
BETTER THAN EZRA; FOUNDER OF PILGRIMAGE MUSIC FESTIVAL

"We're living in unprecedented times. Entrepreneurs, creatives, and other artists have never had more control over their work than they do today. But that also means the old solutions don't always work as well as they once did. Thankfully, there's Jeff Goins's *Real Artists Don't Starve*. This handbook for the new creative economy reveals actionable principles to succeed in today's environment."

—MICHAEL HYATT, *NEW YORK TIMES* BESTSELLING AUTHOR
OF *PLATFORM: GET NOTICED IN A NOISY WORLD*

"This book is your wake-up call, packed with provocative ideas and compelling stories that light the way."

—JONATHAN FIELDS, AUTHOR OF *HOW TO LIVE A GOOD LIFE* AND FOUNDER OF GOOD LIFE PROJECT®

"The myth of the starving artist not only sabotages opportunities for artists, but also keeps society from receiving the gifts of art. Jeff Goins will show you how to make a healthy living from your creative talents, without losing your muse, soul, or morals. If you are an artist, or love one, get this book."

—PAMELA SLIM, AUTHOR OF *BODY OF WORK*

"For centuries, the myth of the impoverished artist has led talented people to opt for a more 'practical' profession. Jeff Goins expertly dismantles this sinister lie, and shows why there has never been a better time to thrive—both personally and professionally—as an artist. Read this book, then pass it on to an artist you love."

—TODD HENRY, AUTHOR OF *THE ACCIDENTAL CREATIVE*

"Finally, a book about art and money that tells it like it is. If you've struggled while trying to make it as an artist, your art isn't the problem—your mindset is. My favorite advice in this book: stay up late and embrace strategic stubbornness. Read it at your own risk!"

—CHRIS GUILLEBEAU, AUTHOR OF *THE $100 STARTUP* AND *THE ART OF NON-CONFORMITY*

"Too many books talk about how to be creative without much practical application to the real world. But this one is different. Jeff Goins shows you how to use your creativity as the weapon it is to make a living and a life for yourself."

—KABIR SEHGAL, *NEW YORK TIMES* BESTSELLING AUTHOR
OF *COINED*; MULTI-GRAMMY AWARD WINNER

"The idea that the artistic and the business mind are separate is just a lie told to keep one side from experimenting with the other. The best artists know their business and the best businesses believe what they do is art. Jeff Goins brings both together into one new way of thinking in this important and necessary book."

—RYAN HOLIDAY, BESTSELLING AUTHOR OF *THE OBSTACLE IS THE WAY* AND *EGO IS THE ENEMY*

Real
Artists
Don't
Starve

Real Artists *Don't* Starve

Timeless Strategies for Thriving
in the New Creative Age

JEFF GOINS

Bestselling Author of *The Art of Work*

HarperCollins
Leadership

An Imprint of HarperCollins

Published by HarperCollins Leadership, an imprint of HarperCollins.

ISBN 978-0-7180-8626-8 (HC)
ISBN 978-0-7180-8628-7 (eBook)
ISBN 978-0-7180-9892-6 (IE)
ISBN 978-1-4002-0102-0 (TP)

Library of Congress Control Number: 2017931116

Printed in the United States of America
18 19 20 21 22   LSC   10 9 8 7 6 5 4 3 2 1

Contents

Introduction

Myth of the Starving Artist

The greater danger for most of us lies not in setting
our aim too high and falling short; but in setting
our aim too low, and achieving our mark.
—Michelangelo Buonarotti

IN 1995, AN AMERICAN PROFESSOR MADE AN UNUSUAL DISCOVERY.

At Syracuse University in Florence, Rab Hatfield was trying to match the scenes of the Sistine Chapel to the dates Michelangelo had painted each of them. Since the artist had received commissions in various installments, the professor thought there might be a paper trail. So he went to the city archives. Surprised at how easy it was to locate five-hundred-year-old bank records, he began reconstructing a more accurate timeline for how the most famous ceiling in the world came to be.

And that's when he saw it.

"I was really looking for something else!" the professor yelled into the phone from his office in Italy, decades later. "Every time I run across something, it's because I was looking for something else, which I consider real discovery. It's when you don't expect it that you really discover something."

With a PhD from Harvard, Professor Hatfield had begun his career at Yale in 1966 before moving to Syracuse University in 1971, and in all that time of teaching art history, he had never encountered anything like this. What he found in those records was not what you would expect to find digging around in the bank account of an artist, even one whose fame would grow with each passing century. "I don't know how much you know about Michelangelo," he told me, "but usually they taught us that he kind of struggled like Vincent van Gogh."

For centuries, this is what historians believed about the great Renaissance master. He was just another Starving Artist, struggling to make ends meet. Michelangelo himself embraced this image, living frugally and often complaining about money. He once wrote in a poem that his art had left him "poor, old and working as a servant of others."

But it turns out he wasn't telling the truth.

When Rab Hatfield dug into those old bank records, the truth about the Renaissance's most famous artist was finally revealed. He was not struggling at all. He was not poor. And he was not starving for his art—a fact we have been getting wrong ever since.

Michelangelo was, in fact, very rich. One record showed a balance of hundreds of thousands of dollars, a rare sum of money for an artist at the time. When he saw those figures, the professor forgot all about the Sistine Chapel. With his curiosity piqued, he went to see if there were more bank records. And there *were* more—many more. In the end, Professor Hatfield uncovered a fortune worth roughly $47 million today, making Michelangelo the richest artist of the Renaissance.

And to this day, this is a story that surprises us.

We are accustomed to a certain story about artists, one that says they are barely getting by. But Michelangelo did not suffer or starve for his work. A multimillionaire and successful entrepreneur, he was in the words of one journalist a "pivotal figure in the transition of creative geniuses from people regarded, and paid, as craftsmen to people accorded a different level of treatment and compensation." In other words, the master sculptor and painter wasn't just some art school dropout struggling for his art. He was a rainmaker.

When I asked Rab Hatfield what Michelangelo's millions meant for us today, he said, "I don't think it means a whole lot." But I disagree. I think this changes everything.

BIRTH OF A MYTH

Two hundred years after Michelangelo died, Henri Murger was born the son of a tailor and concierge in France. Living in Paris, he was surrounded by creative geniuses and dreamed of joining them but grew frustrated with his failure to find financial security.

In 1847, Murger published *Scènes de la vie de bohème*, a collection of stories that playfully romanticized poverty. The result was some literary acclaim, persistent struggle, and an untimely end to a penniless life. The book limped along after the author's death, being adapted first as the opera *La Bohème* and later as a film, eventually achieving widespread acclaim with spinoffs, including *Rent* and *Moulin Rouge*.

Murger's *Scènes* launched the concept of the Starving Artist into the public's understanding as the model for a creative life. To this day, it endures as the picture for what we imagine when we think of the word *artist*. The story of the Starving Artist overshadows the quiet, relatively unknown tale of Michelangelo's success and has become our most popular understanding of what's possible for creative people—which is to say, not much.

Today, we find the remnants of this story nearly everywhere we look. It is the advice we give a friend who dreams of painting for a living, what we tell a coworker who wants to write a novel, or even the tale we tell our children when they head out into the real world. *Be careful,* we say ominously. *Don't be too creative. You just might starve.*

But what we forget is that the story of the Starving Artist is a myth. And like all myths, it may be a powerful story, one we can orient our entire lives around. But in the end, it is still just a story.

THE STORY OF THE STARVING ARTIST IS A MYTH.

Thanks to the power of this myth, many of us take the safe route in life. We become lawyers instead of actresses, bankers instead of poets, and doctors instead of painters. We hedge our bets and hide from our true calling, choosing less risky careers, because it seems easier. Nobody wants to struggle, after all, so we keep our passion a hobby and follow a predictable path toward mediocrity.

But what if you could make a living as an artist? What would that change about the way we approach our work and how we consider creativity's importance in our world today? What would that mean for the careers we choose and the paths we encourage our kids to follow?

In the early Renaissance, artists did not have reputations for being diligent workers. They were considered manual laborers, receiving meager commissions for their work. Michelangelo, however, changed that. After him, every artist began to see a "new pattern, a new way of doing things," in the words of William Wallace, professor of art history at Washington University in St. Louis. Michelangelo "established the idea that an artist could become a new figure in society and have a higher social standing, and also that they could become financially successful."

Michelangelo did not need to starve for his creations, and neither do you. When the painter of the Sistine Chapel amassed an incredible fortune and secured his legacy as one of history's masters, he broke the glass ceiling for future generations. Today, however, his contribution has been all but forgotten. We have bought into the Myth of the Starving Artist, thinking of artists as unfortunate Bohemians who struggle at the lowest end of society.

Rarely do we think of creatives as wealthy or successful, even cracking jokes about the wastefulness of art degrees and theater classes. We have heard how pursuing creativity is not a safe career move, whether that means chasing an interest in literature, music, or some other endeavor. All my life, I heard it from well-meaning teachers, friends, and relatives. The advice was always the same: *Get a good degree, have something to fall back on, and don't quit your day job.*

Creativity, though a nice outlet for self-expression, is not something we think a person should go "all in" on for a career. Because, odds are, you'll starve, right? The truth, though, is quite different. Sometimes, though, an artist *does* succeed: a singer releases a platinum record, an author hits a bestseller list, a filmmaker launches a blockbuster. We tend to dismiss these moments as rare instances of an artist getting lucky or selling out. But what if that wasn't the whole picture?

When we look at history's most famous artists, we see something curious. It's the same thing we observe in the lives of creatives making a living today. When we hear the cautionary tales and warnings about what it means to be an artist, there's an important truth we must embrace:

You don't have to starve.

A New Kind of Artist

In this book, I want to offer a very simple but challenging argument: *Real artists don't starve.* Making a living off your creative talent has never been easier, and to show you it's possible I will share examples of well-known artists, creatives, and entrepreneurs who did not have to suffer to create their best work. And I will also introduce you to a contemporary group of professionals who are experiencing surprising amounts of success in their creative work. Finally, I will try to convince you that the idea of the Starving Artist is a useless myth that holds us back more than it helps us.

Today, with more opportunity than ever to share our work with the world, we need a different model for creative work. The Myth of the Starving Artist has long since overstayed its welcome, and what we need now is a return to a model that doesn't require creative workers to suffer for their art. We need a New Renaissance.

The world needs our work—whether that's an idea for a book, a vision for a start-up, or a dream for a community—and you shouldn't have to struggle to create it. We all have creative gifts to share, and in that respect, we are all artists. But what does it mean to be a "real artist"? It means you are spending your time doing the things that matter most to you. It means you don't need someone else's permission to create. It means you aren't doing your work in secret, hoping someone may discover it someday. The world is taking you seriously.

Do you have to become a millionaire like Michelangelo? Not at all. This is not a book about how to get rich selling art. It is a description of the way many professional artists, creatives, and entrepreneurs have succeeded, and you can join them.

The goal here is to build a life that makes creating your best work not only possible but inevitable. And so, we must exchange this idea of a Starving Artist with a new term: *Thriving Artist*. If you don't want your best work to die with you, you must train yourself to think and live differently than the ways we've been told artists behave. Don't starve for your art. Help it thrive.

Inspired by the Michelangelo story, I was curious to see if there were other artists who were thriving. What I discovered was that not only was a New Renaissance possible, it was already here. I encountered creatives in nearly every field who weren't starving at all. These artists may not have known of Michelangelo's riches, but they embodied his same approach to creative work and followed a similar set of principles I've now captured in this book.

Here they are, the principles every Thriving Artist lives by—the Rules of the New Renaissance:

1. The Starving Artist believes you must be born an artist. The Thriving Artist knows you must become one.
2. The Starving Artist strives to be original. The Thriving Artist steals from his influences.
3. The Starving Artist believes he has enough talent. The Thriving Artist apprentices under a master.
4. The Starving Artist is stubborn about everything. The Thriving Artist is stubborn about the right things.
5. The Starving Artist waits to be noticed. The Thriving Artist cultivates patrons.
6. The Starving Artist believes he can be creative anywhere. The Thriving Artist goes where creative work is already happening.
7. The Starving Artist always works alone. The Thriving Artist collaborates with others.

8. The Starving Artist does his work in private. The Thriving Artist practices in public.
9. The Starving Artist works for free. The Thriving Artist always works for something.
10. The Starving Artist sells out too soon. The Thriving Artist owns his work.
11. The Starving Artist masters one craft. The Thriving Artist masters many.
12. The Starving Artist despises the need for money. The Thriving Artist makes money to make art.

For the rest of this book, we will explore these rules in the context of three major themes: mind-set, market, and money. In each part, we will take a significant step to shift from Starving Artists to Thriving Artists.

First, we will master our mind-set, tackling the internal challenges and conflicts we face to break out of the Starving Artist paradigm. We can't change our lives until we change our minds.

Then, we will master the market, exploring the importance of relationships in creative work and how to usher our art into the world.

Finally, we will master money, looking at what it means to make a living off our work so that we can use money to do better work.

Each chapter is based on one of the twelve rules mentioned above, along with stories and case studies from the hundreds of interviews I conducted with contemporary creatives, artists, and entrepreneurs. The rules represent proven strategies to help you succeed. The more of these you follow, the more likely your success will be.

This book is a manual designed to help you create work that matters. As you encounter the stories and lessons it contains, I hope you are challenged to follow in the footsteps of those who have come before you. I hope you realize that being a Starving Artist is a choice, not a necessary condition of doing creative work, and whether or not you starve is up to you.

And I hope you are emboldened to join the ranks of the New Renaissance, embracing Michelangelo's belief that you can live both a creative life and a prosperous one, declaring to yourself and to the world that real artists don't starve—or at least, they don't have to.

BEING A
STARVING **ARTIST**
IS A CHOICE, NOT A NECESSARY
CONDITION OF DOING

CREATIVE

WORK.

Part 1

MIND-SET

WE FIRST APPROACH OUR ART NOT WITH OUR HANDS BUT WITH OUR minds. We all develop thought patterns and limiting beliefs that prohibit us from being where we want to be in life, and creative work is no exception. Here, we attack those obstacles head on, adopting new ways of thinking, so that we can stop starving and start creating. We must master our mind-set.

Chapter 1

You Aren't Born an Artist

> The Starving Artist believes you
> must be born an artist.
> The Thriving Artist knows
> you must become one.

*I had been my whole life a bell, and never knew it
until at that moment I was lifted and struck.*
—Annie Dillard

ADRIAN CARDENAS GREW UP IN MIAMI, FLORIDA, AS THE SON OF Cuban immigrants. Fleeing the rule of Fidel Castro, the Cardenas family escaped to America, where their son took up the most American of sports: baseball. Soon, Adrian learned he was good at the game, and his talent grew into a dream, which became his ticket to a whole new life. It was an organic process, learning to play. "There's this call and response that goes on," he recalled. "The next step is to play in this league. Do people want you? Yes, sure, so then you're playing in *that* league."

Following that call and response, Adrian advanced in the game, playing all the way through school. In 2006, he won the Baseball America High School Player of the Year award and was drafted out of high school by the Phillies. In 2012, he went to play for the Chicago Cubs, and that was the year that changed everything.

In the majors, Adrian was in the best shape of his life, making more money than he or his immigrant parents ever could have dreamed, building a career based on the rules we know all too well. *Get a good job, do it well, and work hard until you retire.* This was the path Adrian Cardenas was on, and he knew how to walk it. With a signing bonus of nearly $1 million, he was every bit the success story we imagine. It had taken Adrian years to get to this point, and now he was finally enjoying the fruits of his labor. He had everything he had ever wanted.

There was just one problem: he no longer wanted it.

During that first year at Wrigley Field, something felt off. It was a feeling that had been haunting the baseball player for some time. In the minors, players teased him for reading Tolstoy in the locker room. In the majors, he noticed how different his idea of a good time was from that of his teammates. He celebrated getting drafted by entertaining friends with Gershwin numbers on the piano. They celebrated by partying. The more of this life he lived, the more he felt like a misfit, and the more he realized that in following one dream, he'd abandoned another.

When Adrian was a child, his parents insisted on piano lessons in hopes that he might one day attend the Juilliard School in New York. He had long loved the craft of writing and was a devout reader. But those interests now seemed like the dreams of a distant past. Still, he couldn't shake the feeling that maybe he was supposed to do something with these urges and interests. As the pieces of a new story began to knit themselves together, Adrian realized he'd ended up somewhere he didn't belong. Despite achieving everything he thought he wanted, it was time for a new dream. It wasn't too late to quit, start over, and reimagine his life—*was* it?

In 2012, the same year he played his first game in the major leagues, Adrian Cardenas left baseball to tell stories. When things seemed stable and sure for the young athlete, he decided to reinvent himself altogether, which was the scariest but best thing he could have done.

The Rule of Re-creation

Sometimes in life, the script we're given no longer fits the story we want to live. We realize the rules we were following were assigned by someone who did not have our best interests in mind. And now, we must do something about it.

Whether we changed our minds or realized the path we were on wasn't leading where we thought, we all have a choice about who we become. We can go in the direction of what is expected of us. Or, we can enter a world of possibility and reimagine our future.

Now, we come to the first rule of the New Renaissance. I call this the Rule of Re-creation, which says that you are not born an artist. You become one.

At any point in your story, you are free to reimagine the narrative you are living. You can become the person you want to be, even if that means adopting an entirely new identity—or a very old one. This is the moment of decision, when who you are and what you want meet. When we find ourselves here, we must be careful of what we do next, because it could send us down one of two very different paths. This was where Adrian Cardenas found himself when he came to terms with the fact that he had dedicated much of his life to a game he no longer wanted to play. To begin a new journey, he had to let go of what was expected of him.

⇒ YOU ARE NOT BORN AN ARTIST. YOU BECOME ONE. ⇐

As a Cuban American, Adrian was used to feeling caught between two worlds. He was never quite American enough for America and never quite Cuban enough for Cuba. Similarly, he long loved the game of baseball but also loved telling stories. And the more he played professional ball, the more irreconcilable these two worlds felt. Just as his parents had taken a risk in leaving Cuba to reboot their lives, he was caught in a similar tension. If he continued playing baseball, he knew he'd have to dedicate himself to the game, which he wasn't sure he wanted to do. It had gotten to the point where he had to work so hard just to maintain the mechanics of his swing and fielding that it no longer felt meaningful to him.

"It's great to do those things and then be able to feel confident enough to play for forty-five thousand people," he said, "but you ask yourself, 'So what? Why does this matter?'"

When he weighed the options, Adrian realized if he were to continue playing the game, he might never be able to tell the story of his parents' immigration from Cuba. And that scared him more than the possibility of leaving the majors. It was a difficult choice, because he loved the game, but this was a moment of clarity when he knew there were costs on either side. And in the end, art beat baseball. As crazy as it sounds, it was easier for Adrian Cardenas to play Major League Baseball than it was for him to sit down and write a story.

"There's something very satisfying about wrestling with this thing that's much more raw and visceral," he said. "It's equally as hard and challenging as baseball, but much more rewarding."

Shortly after leaving the game, Adrian joined his father on a trip to Cuba, where Juan Cardenas showed his son the locations of multiple escape attempts, as well as the route that finally helped him flee the island. In many ways, the two stories parallel each other. Both generations of men found themselves in seemingly inescapable situations. One was an oppressive regime, the other a "golden handcuffs" situation. For both, they were told by peers that they should comply. Juan was a poet whose poems had gotten him in trouble with the state, and Adrian was an artist whose musings had estranged him from fellow ballplayers. Both men had to do something daring, with everyone around them saying it couldn't be done. But once they decided to follow a new set of rules, they were able to live and tell a whole new story with their lives.

After the trip, Adrian published a series of articles about the experience, sharing his father's escape story. With bylines in the *New Yorker* and on CNN.com as well as a feature in the *New York Times*, the former baseball player is now realizing his dream of telling stories for a living. It took a daring effort to reinvent the person he was becoming, but in the end, it was worth it.

Benefits of Breaking the Rules

If we want to become artists, we are going to have to break some rules. We cannot do just what is expected of us. At some point, we must break away from the status quo and forge a new path. As it turns out, this is how creativity works best.

The famous psychologist Paul Torrance grew up on a farm in Georgia. One of his first jobs was working at a military academy where he saw how students with high energy and a lot of ideas were labeled as "deviant." Something about that bothered him, so he began exploring the connection between misfit behavior and creative potential. Thus began a lifelong study that would help launch a brand-new field of psychology.

Torrance believed creativity could exist in all areas of life and that anyone could be creative. The more research he did, however, the more he discovered how difficult it was to be creative in certain settings, particularly schools. He also observed how creative individuals tended to struggle in systems that forced them to comply to rules they didn't understand. "The creative kids are the ones who rail against the rules the hardest," said Bonnie Cramond, a former student of Torrance, in summary of her teacher's findings. "Creative kids have no patience with ridiculous rules. They don't see any purpose in it." Professor Torrance concluded that following the rules does not produce outstanding creative work. If you aren't willing to be a little deviant, then it's harder to be creative. Sometimes it pays to break the rules.

What, then, does this mean for us in our quest to share our art with the world? There is this idea that artists are born, not made. The Muse kisses you on your forehead at birth, and you spend the rest of your life creating magnificent work. But the reality is that creativity is work, not magic, and those who buck the status quo are far more likely to succeed.

The rules of the Starving Artist told us that if we weren't born with a paintbrush in hand, then we weren't one of the special ones. But these rules no longer serve us. We need something more than the well-intentioned "good luck" from our parents when sharing a dream of writing a novel, becoming an actor, or launching a start-up. We need to know our gifts are here for a reason and that whatever we did before now, we don't have to stay stuck here.

When Adrian Cardenas left baseball, he was breaking a rule, the rule that says you have to do what you've always done, that you can't change things midcareer and do something else. After all, when you have a good thing going, you can't just walk away from it, right? But one year into a career where players make a minimum of half a million dollars a year, the young athlete quit baseball to become an artist, which illustrates an important lesson. Before you can create great art, you first have to create yourself.

Re-creating yourself means letting go of who you were before and accepting a new identity. It means walking away from what people said you should be in exchange for something better. Inevitably, this means we have to break some rules. Maybe they are even the rules of our parents or of society. Maybe they are the rules we gave ourselves. Wherever they may come from, these rules tend to say the same things: "You could never do *that*" and "Who are you to think such things?" We assume where we are in life is where we must remain, but the creative life is a process of possibility, of reimagining what could be. And so we find ourselves on the cusp of transformation. The question to ask ourselves is, are we willing to become our true selves?

Who Do You Think You Are?

All his life, Michelangelo was told he had been born into a noble family. This belief guided his understanding of himself, fueling his ambition to become a successful artist. Wherever he went, he was the disenfranchised aristocrat eager to restore his family name to honor. He knew that if he were going to make it as an artist, he was going to have to make a living; and if he were going to do that, then people were going to need to take him seriously.

BEFORE YOU CAN CREATE GREAT ART, YOU FIRST HAVE TO CREATE YOURSELF.

Given that an artist was considered to be a lowly profession at the time, Michelangelo's choice in vocation was a source of conflict between him and his father. Ultimately, it was a decision that made him very successful, but for many years, it was a hard fight. With the odds against him, what guided the young artist? What made him thrive when so many before him had starved? It was the story he told himself.

"If you grow up believing you're connected to one of the most important families in Europe, and everyone around you believes that, that informs your entire persona and that's how people treat you," said Michelangelo scholar William Wallace. The artist went through life believing he was related to one of the most influential families in Europe, a conviction that, in the words of Wallace, was "profoundly believed by him and all his contemporaries. It was fundamental to the way he looked at life and his art."

This belief in his own nobility guided Michelangelo, shaping his life and paving the route to his success. But here's the interesting part: it wasn't true. He was not actually from noble lineage, a fact that historians discovered years later. What made him succeed was not a genetic predisposition or some cosmic giftedness. It was how he thought of himself.

What we believe about ourselves has a way of coming true—the good *and* the bad. I have had personal experience with this. At twelve years old, I had long hair and was more than a little chubby, wearing baggy jeans and loose shirts to conceal the fact. Puberty was still a few years away, so any masculine features, including facial hair, were practically nonexistent. At a time when peer feedback is at its most brutal point, I was occasionally mistaken for a girl.

That year, I got my first job, delivering newspapers to houses in my neighborhood. After a month on the job, I went door to door collecting dues and met one of my clients, an older gentleman who was retired. As he paid me for a month's worth of work, plus a generous tip, he remarked, "Well, aren't you an enterprising young lady! I have no doubt you're going to be a very successful entrepreneur one day." As I stood there, staring at him blankly, he placed several crisp dollar bills in my hand, smiled, and closed the door.

In the moment of mistaken identity, I was too embarrassed to correct him, and I felt even more awkward doing so afterward, so I just learned to live with it. Taking the less rocky path, I embraced my new identity as a female, letting the "young lady" comments slide. It seemed easier that way. After all, how often did I really have to see this guy? Once a month to collect dues? I could probably live with that. Plus, the money was good.

Over time, though, his comments started to wear on me. After all, is there anything worse for an adolescent boy than to be called a girl? It unnerved me, the fact that he believed something about me that wasn't true. Living in what Thomas Merton calls the "false self," we fall out of alignment with who we are, and I can tell you from experience there is no greater pain than living a lie when the truth is buried deep inside you.

Unable to face the man and tired of delivering papers in the onslaught of Illinois winters, I quit the job. Avoiding the issue seemed the easiest path. Unfortunately, this kind of thing kept happening throughout my adolescence and early adulthood. It took a long time for me to realize I didn't have to assume the identity other people gave me. I could be who I truly was, maybe even change that if I wanted.

There is no greater pain than living a lie when the truth is buried deep inside you.

Years after that first job as a paperboy, I had another job as a marketing director for a nonprofit. During my fifth year working there, though, I realized it was not where I ultimately wanted to be. So I began to call myself a writer, which was something I did for myself but became a way to declare who I was to the world. The more I did this, the more other people believed it, and therefore the more *I* believed it. And over time, it became true.

The reason many of us never self-actualize is because it's easier to play a role in life than it is to become our true selves. It's easier to conform to what people expect than it is to stand out. But this is not the way great art is made, nor is it the way real artists are made.

Eventually, you have to decide who you are. You have to choose your role and own that identity. We don't fake it till we make it. We believe it till we become it.

This is what Michelangelo did at the beginning of his career. He thought like an aristocrat, acted like one, and demanded to be treated like one. By the time the artist died, he was just that: an aristocratic artist whose family name had reached an unprecedented place of prominence. His self-constructed identity gave him, in the words of William Wallace, "a real destiny and purpose in life that was more than just being an artist and making money. He felt like he was . . . building for his family for the future." And because he believed it, he did it.

Take the Right Risks

Once we have embraced who we really are, once we have endeavored to re-create ourselves, what next? How do we take practical steps to start living the life of an artist? Often we think it's the giant leaps that lead to this kind of reinvention, but usually it's a series of small steps.

As a new father and lawyer, John Grisham woke up early every morning, went to his office, and wrote a page of his novel. That was his goal. One page per day for 365 days in a row, without fail. It took three years, but by the end of that time, he had completed the manuscript for his first book, *A Time to Kill.*

The book would eventually go on to be a bestseller, one of many to follow, and in the process Grisham would invent a new genre— the legal thriller. Soon, he would become one of the world's most successful authors, but he did not do this by betting big. He became a writer by stealing away a little time, thirty minutes to an hour each day. That was it. With a growing family and a new career, it would have been reckless to quit law and become a full-time author. In fact, that wasn't even his goal; he was just writing to see if he could do it. He took one step at a time, and three years later he had a book.

More often than not, our creative dreams aren't launched overnight. They are built gradually. When you are in a season of life when you can't dedicate hours a day to your craft, it can feel like you're standing still. But at those times, when the odds are overwhelming and the busyness is suffocating, you still have something to give. The effort may seem small and insignificant, but the work adds up.

Most of us, however, love a good tale of risk and reward. We get a thrill out of seeing people go "all in" on chasing their passions.

But a study from the University of Wisconsin at Madison demonstrated that this is not the wisest way to take a talent and turn it into a career. In 1994, a pair of researchers set out to measure whether business owners were more successful by staying at their day jobs or by leaving them.

The study conducted by Joseph Raffiee and Jie Feng lasted until 2008 and followed five thousand American entrepreneurs who either "took the leap" and quit their day jobs or kept them. And the results surprised them, defying what we might think the typical entrepreneurial success looks like. In the end, the more cautious entrepreneurs ended up being the more successful ones, whereas the risk takers who quit their jobs early were 33 percent more likely to fail.

Sometimes, it's not the big bets that pay off but the small ones that get you the big win. If you don't have to go all in, don't. Why not start with a smaller risk? Most significant change begins with a simple step, not a giant leap. You don't need to see the whole path to know what your next move is; you just need to take the next, right risk. Small changes over time can lead to massive transformation.

MOST SIGNIFICANT CHANGE BEGINS WITH A SIMPLE STEP, NOT A GIANT LEAP.

When I began my career as a writer, I interviewed novelist Steven Pressfield and asked, "When does a writer get to call himself a writer?" "You are when you say you are," he told me. For me, this meant putting the title "writer" on my business cards and e-mail signature and telling others this was now my job, even though it wasn't. Before I expected others to take me seriously, I had to start taking myself seriously. It meant getting up every day and treating my writing like a job. This was a risk, of course, because people could laugh at or try to discourage me, but it felt like the right risk. I wasn't quitting my job or taking a giant leap; I was just taking one small step.

Over time, these steps add up. It may take years for people to recognize your work and the value of it, but this slow and steady route is often better than a big risk that requires you to either succeed immediately or fail. Sometimes, such failure can be hard to recover from, especially when we place too much pressure on our performance and don't give ourselves enough time to practice and prepare for the life of a professional.

If you're waiting for your moment, don't. Start now. If you're wondering if you had to be born to paint or sing or dance, you don't. You just have to choose to become someone else, if the role you're playing isn't the one you wanted. You don't become an artist by moving to New York City without a penny to your name. You become an artist because you decide that's what you're going to be, and then you do the work.

It's a small risk but an important one, and that's always the first risk to take.

When John Grisham finished *A Time to Kill*, he pitched it to forty different publishers who all rejected the book. Unfazed, he started working on a new novel. At this point, he'd had three years of practice and was beginning to understand that the creative life is a series of small steps more than any single giant leap.

While working on his second book, Grisham published his first book with a short run of five thousand copies. When the publisher didn't offer much support, he bought one thousand copies to market the book on his own. While promoting *A Time to Kill*, Grisham finished *The Firm*, which ended up with a major publisher and catapulted his career. It wasn't until he was two bestsellers in to his writing career that he felt confident enough to leave his law practice and pursue writing full time. That's the art of the small bet.

This was what Adrian Cardenas did too. Though he wanted to quit baseball immediately, his mother told him to invest the money he'd made in some property and to make a more gradual transition. The result was a lasting career in art instead of a brief one.

The first step to doing creative work is just that—a step, not a leap or an epiphany—just one small decision that leads to the next one. Sure, some people may risk it all and end up winning, but those are the exceptions to the rule, and that kind of success is often short-lived. The alternative—doing something so small and gradual that it almost looks like you're doing nothing—often leads to much more sustainable success.

You can do extraordinary things when you are patiently persistent.

ORBIT THE HAIRBALL

In various seasons of life, we will encounter systems that may call us to compromise our true selves. When this happens, we must remember that we are never done becoming who we are and these, too, are opportunities to be creative.

For seventeen years, Gordon Mackenzie was a member of Hallmark's contemporary design team, which he called "an unruly, but prodigiously productive stepchild" of a department. This was a division that made money with oddball, humorous products that didn't quite fit into the ethos of Hallmark as a respectable seller of greeting cards. Gordon loved the contemporary design team—it broke just enough rules to keep things interesting—and he would have happily stayed there. But then the unexpected happened.

In 1979, Hallmark's competitor American Greetings landed a Strawberry Shortcake licensing deal. The influx of money for their rival had Hallmark executives shifting company resources toward licensing opportunities, and Gordon was reassigned to the hastily thrown-together Hallmark Properties division. Caught up in the desire to be a high-producing corporate businessman, he pursued money, prestige, and power. He even did the unthinkable and bought a suit.

The promise of prestige clouded Gordon's artistic sensibilities, and before long, he had compromised quality for a paycheck and he knew it. Something had to change. The solution came from his own imagination: a made-up department that would be an escape from the toxic work environment he'd created for himself. It would be a place where he and his creative peers could thumb their noses at bureaucracy, greed, and the status quo.

Translating his vision into a one-page, handwritten proposal, he turned it into a lunchtime pitch to the vice president of Creative. Unsure if the VP would go for it, Gordon had to at least try, but by the end of the meal, his boss said, "We've got to do it."

The Humor Workshop was born, and Gordon's team of twelve set out to operate as no department in the organization ever had. Pretending to pool their money to start a studio in which Hallmark was no longer an employer but a client, the team felt free to create however they wanted. It became a creative paradise for team members, a place where everyone experienced a rebirth within a culture that had grown antagonistic to creative work.

After three years, Gordon was invited back to the corporate headquarters, or "the Big Grey Place" as he called it, where he was given an opportunity to take on a new but unclear role. There was one piece, however, that made the offer irresistible: he could write his own job description. Gordon accepted the position and gave himself the new and unheard-of job title "Creative Paradox."

The title, as well as the position, was a complete fabrication. It came with no job description and no parameters whatsoever. For some, such freedom would have been crippling, but Gordon found it liberating. His office became an idea chamber where he would listen to people's ideas and affirm the ones he liked.

At Hallmark, word began to spread that people could take their ideas to the Creative Paradox and because no one knew where that title sat on the corporate hierarchy, everyone assumed he had the authority to approve any idea that came across his desk. In meetings, when people heard that a certain project had received the Creative Paradox's approval, people were afraid to disagree with it. The truth was that Gordon had no authority at all. "But," he recalled, "as soon as they assumed I had a certain amount of power: I had it."

For the last three of his thirty years at Hallmark, Gordon spent his time as the Creative Paradox. With such a vague title, he was able to orbit the bureaucratic mess, making up new rules as he went. "They were the most enriching, fruitful, productive, joy-filled years of my entire career," he said. "Talk about a paradox."

In his book, Gordon describes his experience at Hallmark as an exercise in "orbiting the giant hairball." The analogy is an apt one for creatives who feel constrained by the systems that surround them. On one hand, we all have the freedom to fly off into our own orbits and be completely independent from the bureaucracies of the world. But when we do this, we end up alone and ineffective in our work, never having the impact we want.

On the other hand, we can do what Gordon did and learn to make the most of these opportunities, reinventing ourselves along the way when the system threatens to rob us of our true selves. The

Thriving Artist knows how to maneuver these hairballs, never becoming a part of them but using the system to do better work.

You're Never Done Becoming Yourself

Over the course of a lifetime, we may find ourselves facing new challenges at every turn, and when we do, we must remember that we are never done becoming who we are. We don't make meaningful art through lateral moves but by constantly challenging ourselves to new heights. We cannot create great art without continuing to create ourselves.

> ## WE CANNOT CREATE GREAT ART WITHOUT CONTINUING TO CREATE OURSELVES.

This work is a process of continuous reinvention. We don't just do it once. It is a journey of becoming, one in which we never fully arrive. "We are all apprentices in a craft where no one ever becomes a master," Hemingway mused.

"Ultimately, creativity is what allowed me to get to the Major Leagues," Adrian Cardenas told me. "But it also took me away from the game, because the passion to do those other things trumped playing in the Major Leagues."

Creativity takes you in and then out and then back in again. It removes you from the system that is encumbering you, gives you a new set of skills, and brings you back to the place you left, this time empowered with a new vision to shape it. This is what happened when Gordon Mackenzie kept reinventing himself, and each reinvention allowed him to do better work than before.

If we want to find our own creative callings, we must be willing to do the same. Our work begins with a decision: Will we assume the role we've been given, or realize it's never too late to become who we are? Life is not fixed; things are always changing. We are either becoming more of our true selves or drifting into a false self.

In the New Renaissance, we get to start over. We get to reinvent and re-create ourselves as much as is necessary, without sticking to a particular path for too long if it doesn't suit our creative needs. Our first job as artists, then, is to venture out, away from what we think we know in search of the new and unexplored. Great artists do this their entire lives, never staying stuck in a single style even when it brings wealth and fame. We must always be striving to reinvent ourselves, continuing to build on who we are and what we've done.

This is the path that Adrian Cardenas is now on. Today, the athlete-turned-artist loves baseball more than ever—but as a hobby. As a student in film school, he's developing his skills to bring his parents' story to the big screen, an opportunity that would never have presented itself had he kept playing baseball. He had to leave the familiar, and through a series of gradual changes, he is now becoming a truer version of himself.

The first step in letting go of the Starving Artist mentality is to let go of who we think we are or must be, even if we have no idea what new identity awaits us. What's out there, however scary it may be, is almost certainly better than staying where we are now.

Art is always found on the fringes, at the edge of our discomfort where true change occurs. It's never too late to start living a new story. You just have to become who you are, taking small steps along the way.

Chapter 2

STOP TRYING TO BE ORIGINAL

The Starving Artist strives to be original. The Thriving Artist steals from his influences.

To be ignorant of what occurred before you were
born is to remain always a child.
—CICERO

WHEN *Sam and Friends* DEBUTED ON MAY 9, 1955, EVERYONE thought they were seeing something new and original. The five-minute TV spot on Channel 4 Washington exploded from the screen with playful puppets, exuberant voices, and a sly sense of humor. It was a shocking departure from the subdued format of variety shows of the day. The short skits immediately connected with both children and adults. It was the kind of debut that defied expectations and shocked viewers, pulling the audience into a whole new world. No one had ever seen anything like it. Or had they?

The puppet show was the TV debut of college students Jim Henson and Jane Nebel, a training ground of sorts for what would later become the Muppets. It was also the culmination of a boyhood dream for Jim, who since the day he begged his parents for a television had been hoping for a chance to appear on TV. Now he was seeing his dream come true. *Sam and Friends* was the young artist's chance to share a new brand of humor with a world that was ready for something more than the traditional puppet show. He and his partner Jane had convinced a local network to take a risk on a couple of unlikely puppeteers who didn't fit the mold, and it was a risk that ultimately paid off. By the end of the series, the couple was making the equivalent of $750,000 a year, and Jim hadn't even graduated college yet.

Who can doubt the impact of *Sam and Friends*? The show would put Jim's and Jane's puppets on the map, leading to what would eventually become an audience of hundreds of millions of fans. And it all started with one big idea. There was just one problem: it wasn't their idea. What audiences thought they saw in *Sam and Friends*—originality, inventiveness, and innovation—were, in fact, all things that had inspired Jim in his then-nineteen years of life.

Like every Thriving Artist, he was not creating something out of nothing. He was stealing from his influences.

The Rule of Creative Theft

The historian Will Durant once wrote, "Nothing is new except arrangement." Even that quote is not new, however, hearkening back to the biblical line that there is "nothing new under the sun." What we perceive as original is often just a rearrangement of what has come before. This is especially true for creativity.

According to researcher Mihaly Csikszentmihalyi, creative work is comprised of five steps: preparation, incubation, insight, evaluation, and elaboration. What we often think of as "creativity" is really the final step, *elaboration*, which requires you to pay attention to several things, including your knowledge of the field and your colleagues. "By interacting with others involved with similar problems," Csikszentmihalyi wrote, "it is possible to correct a line of solution that is going in the wrong direction [and] to refine and focus one's ideas."

In other words, we create not in isolation but with the influence of others around us. So forget the flashes of insight and every other myth you've heard. Creativity is not about being original; it's about learning to rearrange what has already been in a way that brings fresh insight to old material. Innovation is really iteration. We learn from those who have come before us and borrow from their creations to make things the world calls "original." As Picasso has been attributed to saying, "Good artists copy. Great artists steal." Ironically, there are others who have been credited for saying the same thing. Even a quote about stealing is not an original creation.

This work we do is not making things out of nothing. Creative work involves pulling together old ideas and offering new insights on them. In a word, *stealing*—that's what creativity really is. We do not create our way into becoming artists; we rob our way in. "You have to steal," actor Michael Caine once said. "Steal whatever you see."

Today we have countless opportunities to borrow from our influences, both present and past, but how we do this matters. This creative theft is not something you do because you are lazy or undisciplined. Quite the opposite, in fact. The best artists steal, but they do so elegantly, borrowing ideas from many sources and arranging them in new and interesting ways. You have to know your craft so well that you can build on the work of your predecessors, adding to the body of existing work.

This was what Jim Henson was doing when he made his TV debut. He had done his homework. Everything he did had been done before in one way or another, but no one had put it together as he had. He stole from the greats who came before him, and in stealing, he made their work better. When the audience of *Sam and Friends* became captivated by what they thought they were seeing for the first time, they believed the novelty was what made the show a success. But more than that, it was Jim's originality that made the work great, his ability to borrow from so many sources and reassemble them into something marvelous.

Who did Jim Henson borrow from? Well, *everyone*. The puppets came from his grandmother, Sarah Brown, whose sewing skills in the Henson house were unmatched. Her example had inspired Jim to pick up needle and thread at an early age, a skill that enabled him to turn any piece of fabric into a living thing—something that would obviously be invaluable for the rest of his life.

The art of puppetry was something he picked up from Burr Tillstrom, the creator of *Kukla, Fran and Ollie*. Tillstrom won the admiration of both children and adults with his performances, which involved him standing behind a stage with a curtain to conceal his movements while the puppets acted out the skit. It was a simple arrangement; one Jim would borrow from and adapt to suit his needs. Later in life, he would credit Tillstrom for doing more to bring puppetry to TV than he ever did.

And that wry sense of humor came from his mother, Betty, whose wit filled their home with laughter. She would pour a glass of milk for her sons and not stop until they literally said the word "when." Along those lines, the comic strip *Pogo* taught him how comedy could be at once lighthearted and serious.

The unique camera angles were lifted from comedian Ernie Kovacs, a deadpan comic with an intuitive sense of how to shoot film for TV. As entertainers were just beginning to learn the new medium, Kovacs was leagues ahead of them, paying more attention to what the at-home audience was seeing than what the live studio audience saw. Jim learned from Kovacs that you needed to look through the camera to enter the world of your audience and adapt your performance accordingly.

All these influences were absorbed into the work of Jim Henson. What he did was not invent something new but use what had been done before. This is how creativity has always worked. Of course, we all want to be original—no one wants to be accused of being a copy-cat. But the Starving Artist worries about being original, whereas the Thriving Artist knows that stealing from your influences is how you make great art.

This is the Rule of Creative Theft, which says greatness doesn't come from a single great idea or eureka moment. It comes from borrowing other people's work and building on it. We steal our way to greatness.

Such an approach wasn't a smart move just for Jim's and Jane's creative work—it was also a sound business strategy. *Sam and Friends* received enough attention to attract major advertising partners, and soon enough, big brands like Wilkins Coffee and Esskay Meats were lining up to pay for their new brand of humor and in-your-face gags.

One particular spot featured two of their earliest puppets talking about Wilkins Coffee. In the brief sketch, the cheerful Willkins asks his friend if he's getting on the Wilkins Coffee bandwagon, and his curmudgeonly companion, Wontkins, says, "Never!" He then gets run over by a passing bandwagon. Simple bits like that were earning the puppet-making duo enough money that this side gig of theirs soon became a full-time career.

Turns out, it really does pay to steal—when you do it the right way.

There was nothing dishonest or illegal about what Jim and Jane were doing. This borrowing of ideas is the kind of "theft" that

Thriving Artists have been practicing for centuries, and it's what you will have to do if you want your art to make it too.

STUDY THE GREATS WHO CAME BEFORE

There is an old Irish myth about a sixth-century monk named Columcille who steals a manuscript from an abbot to copy it. When the abbot discovers the theft, he demands the young monk return the original as well as the reproduction.

Columcille refuses, and the case is brought before the high king, who commands the monk to return both documents. This ruling infuriates the monk, who impulsively tells his father who also happens to be a king. This causes a battle that leaves the abbot dead and the young man plagued with guilt. The young monk is then banished from Ireland, along with twelve companions, and he lives out his exile on Iona, a small island off the coast of Scotland.

At Iona, Columcille spends the remainder of his days paying penance through missionary journeys and doing the very thing that got him kicked out of his country in the first place—copying ancient documents. Soon, Iona becomes a center of Celtic Christianity and a refuge of western culture, one of only a few sites where art and culture are preserved while barbarian hordes destroy much of it, ushering in the Dark Ages.

The documents copied by Columcille and his monks are saved from destruction and preserved for posterity, thus rescuing western culture from near annihilation. But how did they do this? They copied manuscripts of ancient documents, which they inherited from the Romans. And the Romans stole much of their culture and art from the Greeks. And the Greeks, of course, borrowed from each other—Sparta from Athens and vice versa. On and on it goes. This is how cultures are made: you copy what has come before you, and you build upon it. You make it better.

There is a secret every professional artist knows that the amateurs don't: being original is overrated. The most creative minds in the world are not especially creative; they're just better at rearrangement. In order to do that, they have to be familiar with their influences. They have to study before they steal. Yes, before you become an artist, you must become a thief; but even before you do that, you must first become a student.

Michelangelo's first commission was a swindle. An art dealer approached him with a request to create a statue and make it look old. The goal was to pass off the work as an original from Roman antiquity, selling it to Cardinal Raffaele Riario, the grandnephew of Pope Sixtus IV and avid art collector of antiquities. At the time, statues like this were appearing all over Italy, so from a strategy standpoint, it was a smart move: hire a talented sculptor to create an authentic-looking statue, rough it up, and sell it to the highest bidder.

BEFORE YOU BECOME AN ARTIST, YOU MUST BECOME A THIEF.

The ruse worked, at least for a while. Cardinal Riario bought the statue, adding it to his collection; however, the deception didn't last long. He discovered the sculpture was fake and returned it to the dealer. What happened next, though, was even more surprising than the forgery itself. The cardinal hired Michelangelo, becoming the artist's first patron in Rome. Riario was not angered by the deception; he was impressed.

During the Renaissance, apprentices were taught to copy their masters' work so precisely that the copies were indistinguishable from the originals. Being able to reproduce an earlier work was not something to be ashamed of—it was a point of pride. In the words of author Noah Charney, it was "a sign of ability, not duplicity" to be able to copy the work of a master artist. So when a young Michelangelo re-created a work from Roman antiquity and sold it to a collector, it boosted his reputation. The great artist knew better than to try to be original. He stole from the past to create the present, and the forgery earned him not only a valuable patron but a reputation as a great artist.

To pull this off, Michelangelo had to possess tremendous patience to study the work of his predecessors and then be able to mimic it so precisely. Such discipline is all but lost in our world today. We are far too impatient, too eager to show the world what we have to offer, too unwilling to take the time to learn the fundamentals of a craft. We would rather create our masterpieces and build our reputations now than endure the tedium of what the masters can teach us. Such an act requires humility, the spirit of a student. But the fact remains that if you want to be great, you must be willing to commit to such efforts.

The ability to copy the work of another artist was not necessarily rare at the time of Michelangelo's forgery. The Renaissance itself was a forgery, made possible by the rediscovery of ancient Roman architecture and artwork, sculptures that were thought to have been lost in the Dark Ages. Great artists of the time were robbing from their predecessors, copying Greek and Roman art forms, repurposing them for a new age. But in that translation, they didn't just copy the past. They built upon it, made it better, and ushered in a new era of art.

Today we live in a world we do not deserve, an age that is the product of previous generations' hard work. This is true of every generation, but especially true today when so many resources and tools are readily at our disposal. Michelangelo and his contemporaries had a similar embarrassment of riches during the Renaissance. But they did not passively receive the opportunities they were given; they recognized and used them. They studied the work of their teachers, mastering their techniques, copying the work that came before and rearranging it to create something the world would call new.

And such is the case for us now, in this New Renaissance. If we want to create work that will stand the test of time, we must honor the legacies we've received. We must become students before we become masters.

Begin as a Copycat, End as a Master

Not only should you steal from the masters who came before you centuries ago, you can also copy your peers. That's what Twyla Tharp did. Since 1965, Tharp has been practicing and teaching the art of dance. During her fifty-year career, she has created more than 130 dances for the Joffrey Ballet, New York City Ballet, Paris Opera Ballet, London's Royal Ballet, American Ballet Theatre, and her own company. She has also won two Emmy awards, a Tony Award, and the MacArthur Fellowship. Today she is considered one of America's foremost choreographers.

If all this sounds like the work of a creative genius, then you're not getting the whole picture. In 2003, Tharp admitted in her book *The Creative Habit* that she is not as original as people think. She is, in fact, a thief. Everything Tharp teaches, in one way or another, comes from something she copied from someone else.

When she started dancing in New York, the dancer dedicated herself to studying every great dancer who was working at the time. She patterned herself after these professionals, learning what she could from them, copying their every move. "I would literally stand behind them in class," she said, "in copying mode, and fall right into their footsteps. Their technique, style, and timing imprinted themselves on my muscles."

Tharp understood that honing her dance skills would begin not with an original technique but by copying what others were doing. She imitated the greats and after years of study created a style that was all her own—at least, that's what people thought. "That's the power of muscle memory," she wrote. "It gives you a path toward genuine creation through simple re-creation." The way you establish your authority in a certain field is by mastering the techniques of those who are already authorities. And what eventually emerges over time is your own style.

For generations, writers have done something similar in copying the words of their favorite authors verbatim. Hunter S. Thompson did this with the work of his idol, F. Scott Fitzgerald, when he wrote out the pages of *The Great Gatsby* to get a feel for "what it was like to write that way." He also admitted in an interview to stealing more words and phrases from the Bible than from any other source, because he liked the way they sounded. Great artists do not try to be original. They copy the work of both masters and peers—word by word, stroke by stroke, they mimic what they admire until those techniques become habitual. "Skill gets imprinted through action," Twyla Tharp said. We create by copying, and as we do, the skill becomes embedded into our memory.

When I began my career as a writer, I wanted to find my voice. Whenever I tried to write in what felt like my style, though, it wasn't good. Inevitably, the writing would drift into the voice of whatever book I was reading. For a long time, I thought real writers did something different. They must have been born with innate talent, some style that was just waiting to get onto the page. Turns out, that's not true. We find our voice by mimicking the voices of others.

Great artists do not try to be original. They copy the work of both masters and peers.

We are all borrowing ideas from someone. As Austin Kleon wrote, "A good artist understands that nothing comes from nowhere. All creative work builds on what came before. Nothing is completely original." When we steal like this, we end up creating a style that is all our own. And so, creative theft becomes a gift that we first receive and then give back to the world. This kind of stealing is how an artist remembers for herself and her audience the greatness that has come before. It is a gift to everyone who witnesses your work.

Twyla Tharp embodies an important truth about creative work. You are not an artist because you steal. You steal because you are an artist. In her case, she improved on the work that she was borrowing from others so much because she knew she had to create. And intuitively, she understood that she did not yet possess the skill to make it. So she studied, then she practiced, and ultimately she created something the world had never seen. This is different from the work of a true thief, an unoriginal hack who doesn't know how to pull the work of others into her own routine and make it her own.

The difference between an artist and a copycat is that the artist builds on the work she has received and the copycat only mimics it. Yes, we all start by doing what others have done, but those who master their crafts don't stop there. They keep copying until the techniques become internalized. Then and only then can you create something the world calls "original."

HONOR AMONG THIEVES

There are moral hazards to this, of course, situations to be aware of so we don't misapply this concept of creative theft. At some point, someone will come along who rips off your work and tries to pass it off as his own. But that's not *creativity*. It's cowardice. How do you create something meaningful and original without being a copycat? There is a code of conduct every Thriving Artist follows—the right way to steal—and we would be wise to follow it.

Creative work requires a careful eye for good work. You have to notice the excellence from which you will steal, and this is easier said than done. We must study the right influences, the ones who are pushing the bounds of what's possible with their craft, the true masters. This is what Jim Henson was doing all those hours staring at the television, watching comedians and puppet masters, while sewing with his grandmother and reading comics. It's what Twyla Tharp did when she mimicked the moves of all those dancers.

As you watch and learn and eventually borrow from these influences, remember to do so in a way that honors them. Let your influences know you are learning from them and that they are inspiring you. Help them understand your motive, which is to build on the work, not pass it off as your own. And as much as possible, cite your sources, giving credit where credit is due. This won't discredit you. It will likely endear you to your influences and your audience. Like Michelangelo, showing your ability to copy others' work will prove that you did your homework.

When you steal, don't just copy and paste the work of your predecessors. Once you have mastered the form, bring those influences together in a new way. Curate before you create. If you do this well, you won't be merely cribbing other people's work and passing it off as your own. You will be building on it and making it better.

Far too many creatives have gotten lost in the pursuit of originality and never created anything significant. But that's not the way of the Thriving Artist. When *Sam and Friends* aired for the final time in 1961, Jim and Jane Henson, who were now married, were perfectly positioned for what would come next. Their career would be filled with more daring exploits—*The Muppets*, *Sesame Street*, *Fraggle Rock*—and a creative legacy for generations to come. Soon they would find themselves giving back to the world of entertainment from which they had so liberally borrowed years before. But now they would not be the ones doing the stealing; they would be the ones being robbed. Because they dared not to be original and instead built on others' work in new and interesting ways, the world will not forget their work.

Creativity starts with stealing, but it does not end there. The creative process, when done right, culminates in something so interesting, that others are now compelled to steal from *you*. That's when you know you've done your job: you are no longer the thief but the one being robbed.

CREATIVITY

STARTS WITH STEALING,

BUT IT DOES NOT

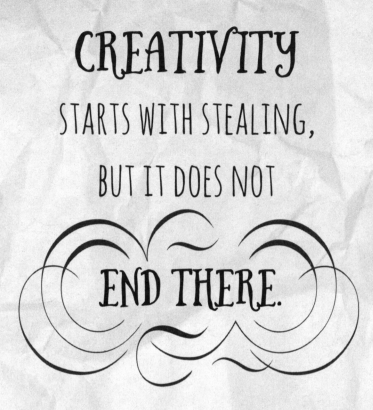

END THERE.

Chapter 3

Apprentice Under a Master

The Starving Artist believes talent is enough.
The Thriving Artist apprentices under a master.

Of such importance is early training.
—Virgil

LIKE A LOT OF PEOPLE, TIA LINK WENT TO COLLEGE BUT DIDN'T KNOW what she wanted to do afterward. Many of her friends were going to law school, which sounded promising. Even if you didn't want to be a lawyer, a law degree could be very versatile, they said.

"As it turns out," she recalled, "that's totally not true. You can be . . . a lawyer."

Nonetheless, she followed her friends' advice and attended Stanford Law. After law school, she went to work for a big firm and soon found herself exhausted by the work. She took some time off to travel, hoping to go into another career when she returned, something—anything—other than law. Little did she know, however, her first career was just preparation for what was to come. And all of it would soon become useful to where she was headed.

When she got back from her travels, Tia ended up back in law, joining a high-frequency trading law firm on Wall Street. It was there she met her second husband, Ben, with whom she eloped, but the new marriage quickly began to crumble. At that point, the young lawyer took a step back to evaluate her life, trying to understand her part in the things that had transpired and why she was so "desperately unhappy" in her day-to-day life. Her job wasn't fulfilling her, and she was coming home expecting a crumbling relationship to make her happy. It wasn't working. None of it was.

Meanwhile, there was something she had always wondered about: acting. As a child, Tia loved performing; she had been so moved by some of her favorite movies that she couldn't help but wonder what it might be like to affect others in the same way.

"I had no idea if I would be any good at it," she said. "I had no idea if I would even like it."

But still, she had to try. Just for fun, Tia took a few acting classes to see what they were like.

After her very first class, she was in love. "It was like, this is where I'm supposed to be," she said.

Everything started to make sense. Tia hadn't been training to become a lawyer, not really. Law school was preparation for an entirely different vocation, though not entirely unlike that of being a lawyer. Without realizing it, Tia was training to be an actor. And now she was beginning to realize a lifelong dream she didn't even know she had.

"So much of what has come before has helped me succeed now," she said. "As a lawyer, you learn everyone is faking it. I learned the appearance of confidence."

Her transition to acting was anything but smooth. She had worked so long in a world that was logical and calculated that it was hard to dream again. Everything anyone had ever told her about being creative came rushing back to her. Foremost was that you don't succeed. An inner voice kept saying, "You're crazy to think this is something you could do. You're too old to start something like this."

The truth, though, is that her apprenticeship began as soon as she made the decision to become an artist. She was already on the path. She just needed to take the next step.

There was little logic to Tia's curiosity about acting. Because of that, she didn't know how to proceed. *Are you really sure you want to do this?* she kept asking herself.

It was at this point she could have gone all in on a crazy idea, or she could have been paralyzed with fear. Fortunately, she did neither. Tia took her time, building a bridge in the direction of her dream, doing both acting and law for a couple of years, using whatever spare time she had.

It was an informal apprenticeship that she designed herself. It began gradually, with a few auditions here and there while continuing to practice law, but the more she pursued acting, the more she liked it and the easier the gigs came.

When I spoke with Tia, she was stepping out of a rehearsal in New York City. Today she is a full-time actor, and in the past year alone, she's done fifteen films, a fact that still surprises her.

"It remains absolutely crazy to me," she said, "that even now acting is my job, it doesn't feel like work. There's this thing that gives me so much pleasure and so much joy."

What got her there was not some lofty dream. It was gradual and persistent action in the right direction. She learned how to be an apprentice.

THE RULE OF APPRENTICESHIP

When we think of creative success, we tend to think in terms of extremes. You either "make it" or you don't. You "leap and the net appears," or it doesn't. But the truth is a little more complicated.

We love to praise the "Big Break," that wonderful moment when the stars align and serendipity visits you, making you an instant success. We wait for such moments, even long for them. But here's the truth: the Big Break is a myth.

Of course, we all get lucky at some point, but luck can be a fickle thing and nearly impossible to replicate. When those special moments come, we can embrace them, but we should never expect them. Creative success is far more often the result of hard work and perseverance. Starving Artists wait for their Big Breaks. Thriving Artists become apprentices in their crafts.

This is what Tia Link was doing, albeit unknowingly, all those years in law school and after. She was learning the art of apprenticeship. By design, apprenticeship is hard. It's supposed to be; that's why so few people endure it.

As Tia said, "The work ethic certainly helps. There's definitely an opinion about actors that they're sort of lazy, lying around waiting for roles, and I can tell you I work longer hours than I ever have."

What does an apprentice do? Whatever is needed. Becoming an apprentice is a choice, an attitude you start practicing today. The marks of a good apprentice are patience, perseverance, and humility.

You are *patient*, because you realize that though your big moment may not come today, if you put the work in, you will eventually see the results.

You *persevere*, because you know this will not be easy and the odds are stacked against you. But if you keep going, you will outlast the majority who quit at the first few signs of trouble.

You are *humble*, because you know how far you still have to go, and this attitude will earn the attention of masters who will want to invest in you and see you succeed.

Not only does an apprentice not give up—they do what no one else is willing to do. It's hard, thankless work, but if you embrace it, in the end you will be better for it. The moment we begin to believe we deserve success is the very moment it will elude us.

We cannot wait for our lucky breaks. We must continually be earning. Luck may get you a break, but skill and a willingness to keep going are what will allow you to keep going.

Apprenticeship may come in many forms, but one thing is certain: it must happen. You cannot become great on your own. You need help. The world doesn't need more amateurs subscribing to a "fake it till you make it" ideology. We need more masters. The sushi chef who practices for a decade before opening his own restaurant. The golfer who endures thousands of hours serving as someone else's caddy. The musician who studies under a pop star for the greater part of a decade. Such experiences are not fun, but they are invaluable training for the future. We must always be practicing, always earning our stripes.

Before we become masters, we must first become apprentices.

APPROACH THE MASTER WITH BOLDNESS

When the young Michelangelo approached Domenico Ghirlandaio, the famous Florentine artist, he must have had a lump in his throat. Michelangelo was barely a teenager and was about to ask one of Florence's most fashionable painters to train him. What's more, the boy's father, Lodavico, was pressuring his teenage son to be the family's breadwinner.

BEFORE WE BECOME MASTERS, WE MUST FIRST BECOME APPRENTICES.

In what must have been a monumental moment for both men, Michelangelo met Ghirlandaio with a combination of fear and respect. Many young Florentines would have been honored to even meet the man, but the boy wanted more. As the story goes, he not only had the audacity to request an apprenticeship from the master but he also asked to be paid.

This was outrageous. In the Renaissance, apprentices did not get compensated. If anything, they often *paid* their way through such an education because of the opportunity. Anyone in Ghirlandaio's studio witnessing the request surely stared in abject horror. Whatever the master must have felt at first—outrage or amusement—he surprised everyone, maybe even Michelangelo, with his willingness to accept the offer.

Michelangelo assisted Ghirlandaio in whatever his master needed. Perhaps just as important as the technical skills he developed in the studio, he also learned what it meant to *be* an artist of such stature: the responsibilities of running a studio, the challenges of managing apprentices, the social dynamics of dealing with patrons. This is most of what an apprenticeship is: watching, listening, and being present in the process. You experience by doing, and you internalize those lessons.

And what must it have been like for Ghirlandaio to take on Michelangelo? Here was a young man who stood out from the rest of the group. He was older than the other apprentices by a year or two. On top of that, Ghirlandaio was paying him! Every time Ghirlandaio gave the boy an assignment or saw him walking around the studio, he must have remembered—here was the boy who had the audacity to ask.

In Michelangelo's free time, he was allowed special access to Ghirlandaio's drawings and paintings; he was free to copy them and learn his master's technique. And why not? Wouldn't you give your attention to a pupil who clearly had the boldness and ability to rise above his peers? Wouldn't such a student be hard to ignore? When the master saw the apprentice's rendition of his own work, Ghirlandaio remarked that Michelangelo's were as good as the originals. How could such a thing be possible, though, if Michelangelo had never apprenticed before?

Becoming an apprentice begins with your mind-set. Long before entering Ghirlandaio's studio, Michelangelo was practicing. He was not waiting for his Big Break; he was doing the work. That meant learning from whomever he could from an early age. He knew he wanted to be an artist and that he could not become great on his own, no matter how talented he might be. No amount of natural ability can compete with diligent practice. He had relatives who worked in the quarry every day and he was able to familiarize himself with stone—a skill that would be invaluable to him later in life. He adopted the attitude of a student, learning from anyone who could teach him.

About a year after Michelangelo's apprenticeship with Ghirlandaio began, the patron Lorenzo de Medici requested two of Ghirlandaio's students to be assigned to the Medici palace as artists in residence. Who came to mind other than the audacious young man who had the boldness to ask and the ability to act? The young artist's time with the master was short but significant, and one that ultimately transformed him into Florence's most prominent artist.

When Michelangelo moved to the Medici household, he studied under Bertoldo di Giovanni, an artist who had learned from the great Donatello. The young artist found himself in the company of greatness. Lorenzo de Medici hosted regular dinner parties that included prominent figures from society such as Niccolo Machiavelli. Once again, Michelangelo made himself a student, soaking up every lesson he could and applying it to his art.

Certainly we cannot overlook the importance of skill in the practice of apprenticeship. But skill is not enough to earn the attention of an influencer—you must be teachable, demonstrating not only your ability but your potential.

This is where boldness comes in, not just in making a request for an apprenticeship but in the willingness to do what must be done.

> ## SKILL IS NOT ENOUGH TO EARN THE ATTENTION OF AN INFLUENCER—YOU MUST BE TEACHABLE.

Being an apprentice is not just about making big asks but being diligent enough to take the work seriously and continue growing. What will make you stand out from the crowd is not just the audacity to ask for help but the humility to learn and act.

APPRENTICESHIP TODAY

During the Renaissance, traditional apprenticeships lasted about a decade. By the time an apprentice was done studying under the master, seven years had passed. During the following three years an apprentice became a journeyman and struck out on his own to prove his worth to the world.

This is a far cry from the standard summer-long internship college students experience.

It's worth noting that very few apprentices made it to the "master" level. The difference between someone who made it and someone who did not ultimately came down to two factors: who helped them and how hard they worked. If they had a good master, they had an advantage; they knew someone who could help them find the right social connections to succeed. And if they did not, or if they didn't apply themselves, they were in a tough spot. In the end, perseverance paid off.

But that was a long time ago. How, if at all, does apprenticeship work today? For starters, it's a lot less formal than in the past. Make no mistake, though: apprenticeship is still alive and well, albeit with a new form.

The first step in an apprenticeship is to find a master worth studying. When you find such a person, consume as much of their work as possible. Read everything they've written, watch everything they do, and buy whatever they might be selling. Your goal is to familiarize yourself with their work.

Then do exactly what they say. Follow their advice, apply their principles, enact their method. Do this first without their knowing. Do whatever you can to model your skill after theirs. Learn the master's style so well they can't help but be wowed, and don't be afraid to show your skill. They may find this endearing and be more likely to be drawn to you, eager to help you.

This is when you ask for their help, their input, their advice. Not before. First become a case study, then ask for help. Don't "pick their brain." Show them that you've done your homework and have put what they've modeled to good use, and now you want more.

This is what Michelangelo did when he proved himself as a

worthy apprentice, someone who would multiply Ghirlandaio's investment of time. It's what good apprentices do. By becoming a case study, you become the ideal champion of their work, promoting everything they do simply by embodying it and broadcasting it to the world, which only serves to strengthen the master's reputation.

FIRST BECOME A CASE STUDY, THEN ASK FOR HELP.

Tia Link spent three years at a job she didn't like, because it afforded her the opportunity to apprentice in her true craft. The fact of the matter is these things take time, and when we try to rush the process, we end up missing valuable lessons along the way.

ENDING THE APPRENTICESHIP

For all the perks of apprenticeship, they aren't supposed to last forever. At some point, you must graduate; you must end the apprenticeship and strike out on your own. If you never do this, you end up with a relationship in which you never create anything original, and it all becomes derivative, anemic work. Plus, apprenticeships don't usually pay much, if at all, so if you become stuck in one, you can end up starving.

There comes a time when all the planning, all the preparation, doesn't prepare you for the next moment, the moment in which you have to take your work seriously enough to succeed at it. When you are being called to that next level, you must respond appropriately. At times like these, you must become a little desperate, which describes Tia Link's state of mind when she was on the verge of quitting her law career to become an actor.

As she put it, "I felt 60 percent excited to finally be following my dreams, 10 percent relieved just to be out of my lawyer job, 20 percent terrified I had made a big mistake, and 10 percent nervous about being poor!"

So what did she do? Did she quit her job and not look back? Not at all. That would have been foolish. She did something better, something we all must do. She entered a season of apprenticeship and chased her dream for three years while still holding down a full-time job.

When you realize the career you're in isn't where you ultimately want to be, you may feel a similar sense of desperation.

We tend to see desperation as a vice, something to avoid. When someone is desperate, we can sense it, and it repels us. But there is another kind of desperation, the kind that says, "If this doesn't work, I will find another way." And that kind of desperation translates to passion, a powerful tool when directed at the right target.

When that time comes, ask yourself, *Have I finished my apprenticeship yet?*

When Tia Link, the lawyer-turned-actress, finally left her job, she didn't have all the answers, but she knew it was time to move on. When she told her boss that she wanted to take a shot at acting full time, she assured her boss that she would stick around until as many things as possible were properly transitioned.

But, Tia was quick to note, she couldn't stay on indefinitely because, "I needed to get busy living."

The attorney part of her apprenticeship was over, and now it was time to go pro in her commitment to becoming an actress. The job that at times had plagued her was, in its own way, a form of training. All her years of practicing law had prepared her for what was to come. And it was only then, in that transition, she realized she'd been training with the masters all along. Now, she was qualified to become one herself.

Tia quit law just before her thirty-fifth birthday. In her first year of acting, she did at least five commercials, filmed a full-length movie, acted in three short films, and started a couple of new classes.

"I just feel lighter," she told me over the phone, in between auditions. "I feel happier. I don't pick up my phone and feel anxiety wash over me about what work e-mail will come through. That's been the biggest change: the anxiety lifting from every second of every day."

Becoming an actress was a choice that surprised everyone in Tia's family, including herself. "I have never ever considered myself a creative person," she told me. For years, she pursued law because it was safe.

"I would've loved to leave earlier," she said, "but I didn't know what I would leave *to*. We, as a society, are not really set up to give people a chance to explore other things in a safe way that lets them say, without judgment or fear, 'I'd just like to try this other thing for a little bit.'"

When I asked Tia when she knew it was the right time to become an actor, she said, "There is no right time. Finally, it just made more sense than it didn't."

It's an inspiring story, but not a traditional one as we are inclined to think such tales should go. Rather, Tia Link's story is one of unexpected apprenticeship, involving years of effort— late nights of rehearsal and early mornings back at the day job. Of course, this was just a season, but a difficult one no less. There was little magic associated with this time and very few breaks, if any. What Tia experienced was a typical apprenticeship. And you should expect nothing less in your own creative journey.

Remember this: apprenticeship requires three important traits: patience, perseverance, and humility.

You must be courageous enough to reach out to a master but at the same time hardworking enough not to waste his time. When things don't go according to plan, do what must be done. And when it doesn't work out, be persistent. Keep showing up, regardless of the outcome. Opportunities may come and go, but in the end, hard work is all we can measure.

OPPORTUNITIES MAY COME AND GO, BUT IN THE END, HARD WORK IS ALL WE CAN MEASURE.

Artists starve because they think they can make it on their own, ignoring the need for a teacher. Thriving Artists, on the other hand, are both humble enough to admit their need and audacious enough to seek it out. Great work is not a result of luck but of a willingness to become an apprentice.

---------- *Chapter 4* ----------

HARNESS YOUR STUBBORNNESS

⇒ THE STARVING ARTIST IS STUBBORN
ABOUT EVERYTHING.
THE THRIVING ARTIST IS STUBBORN
ABOUT THE RIGHT THINGS. ⇐

We are stubborn on vision. We are flexible on details.
—JEFF BEZOS

AS A YOUNG MAN, F. SCOTT FITZGERALD RESISTED THE TEMPTATION to marry early in life because of his determination to become a great writer. Despite his reluctance, however, he fell in love with a young woman while he was stationed as a soldier in Montgomery, Alabama, in 1918.

The youngest of six children from a prominent Southern family, Zelda Sayre was also reluctant to marry an unpublished writer whose career prospects were uncertain. A month after meeting her, Fitzgerald received a rejection letter from a publisher for a book manuscript he had submitted, encouraging him to revise the work and submit again. He and Zelda began writing letters to each other, but she continued to see other men.

After the war ended and Fitzgerald was discharged from the military, he moved to Manhattan, eager to prove himself both as a suitor and writer. After being turned down for a position at a newspaper, he went to work at the advertising agency Barron Collier, where he composed trolley-car advertisements for thirty-five dollars a week.

He never gave up his dream of being a writer, however, spending most nights writing stories, poems, and jokes—whatever might earn some money. Zelda remained unimpressed by his lack of success, which only seemed to further drive him toward it.

During that time, Fitzgerald acquired an important trait. It was something that would go hand in hand with being a writer, one we often overlook in the pursuit of creative work today. In the spring of 1919, the writer put this resource to great use, writing 19 stories and receiving 122 rejection slips. He accumulated so many letters of refusal that the walls of his rented room were covered with them.

The rejection did not dissuade him, though; it spurred him on. He had a secret weapon all artists possess: stubbornness. For the young writer, this was a season of failure and disappointment, but his stout refusal to quit helped him endure. He just would not give up—not on love and not on writing.

ALL ARTISTS HAVE A SECRET WEAPON: STUBBORNNESS.

When Fitzgerald wrote to Zelda informing her that his first novel, *This Side of Paradise*, had been accepted by Scribner's, she finally agreed to marry him. The wedding took place a week after the novel's publication.

For the next four years, the author made stubbornness his ally, publishing another novel and numerous short stories to literary acclaim and commercial success. The same quality that had helped him win over his wife had made him one of America's preeminent young writers, earning the modern equivalent of two thousand dollars per short story and five hundred thousand dollars a year. Stubbornness, it seems, served Fitzgerald well.

In 1923, when he began writing his third novel, the author could not have been more confident about his new project. "Artistically," he wrote in a letter to his editor, Max Perkins, "it's head [and] shoulders over everything I've done." The more he worked, though, the more self-conscious he grew. Of his stories, he told a friend, "they grow worse and worse."

He turned inward and obsessed over every detail of his work, which began to erode his confidence. As the new novel approached publication, Fitzgerald grew nervous. "*The Great Gatsby* is weak," he said of the title, casting his vote instead for *On the Road to West Egg* or *The High-Bouncing Lover.* He worried the book wouldn't appeal to women, that the reviews would be bad, and that it wouldn't sell well enough to pay the publisher back his advance.

As Fitzgerald expected, almost all these fears came true. *The Great Gatsby* was published on April 10, 1925, with one New York paper headlining its review: "F. Scott Fitzgerald's Latest a Dud." The rest of the literary world was equally critical, with H. L. Mencken calling it "no more than a glorified anecdote" and referring to the author as "this clown." A bit more bluntly, Ruth Snyder wrote, "We are quite convinced after reading *The Great Gatsby* that Mr. Fitzgerald is not one of the great American writers of today." *Gatsby* did not achieve the success its author had hoped for, selling fewer than half as many copies as any of his previous novels.

The failure crushed him.

Afterward, the author found it even more difficult to write. His personal life fell apart, too, when he admitted Zelda to a mental hospital in 1936 and was left to provide for their daughter on his own. Never fully recovering from the disappointment of his failure, he moved to Hollywood to write screenplays, a decision he later regretted. He struggled with alcoholism for most of his adult life and died of a heart attack in 1940 at the age of forty-four.

At the time of Fitzgerald's death, *The Great Gatsby* was practically out of print and nowhere to be found in bookstores. His last royalty check was for thirteen dollars, most of which was from copies the author had purchased himself. A once-promising novelist ended his career doing what he considered hack work and went to the grave thinking himself a failure.

STRATEGIC STUBBORNNESS

We all need the ability to persevere and maintain passion for long-term goals despite adverse circumstances—or what Angela Duckworth calls "grit."

In a popular research paper, Duckworth wrote that grit "entails working strenuously toward challenges, maintaining effort and interest over years despite failure, adversity, and plateaus in progress. The gritty individual approaches achievement as a marathon; his or her advantage is stamina. Whereas disappointment or boredom signals to others that it is time to change trajectory and cut losses, the gritty individual stays the course."

The story of F. Scott Fitzgerald is a sad one, but did it have to be? Per Duckworth's definition, what the man seemed to lack at the end of his life was grit. Perhaps blinded by his own success or distracted by details, the young writer was unprepared for the rejection that would soon follow. Lacking the perseverance to push through the inevitable plateaus of a literary career, a failure practically destroyed him.

He was stubborn in the wrong things, losing the initial grit that had allowed him to persevere through early rejection. He forgot the big picture, which is that an artist's job is not to be perfect but to be creating. This is a common pitfall among creatives, especially those of us working on what we believe to be our magnum opus. The work consumes us, leading to an unhealthy focus on the small things.

AN ARTIST'S JOB IS NOT TO BE PERFECT BUT TO BE CREATING.

When Fitzgerald published *The Great Gatsby*, he had high hopes for his novel. Because of these expectations he fixated on the details, and when it flopped he was devastated. We need something to protect us against such disappointments, a way to steel ourselves against the inevitable critique of our work.

The way we do this is not just by being stubborn about anything and everything, but through strategic stubbornness. We must not only use our stubbornness to succeed—we must harness it and apply it toward the right things, turning it into tenacity. Otherwise, what helps us succeed can also be the source of our undoing. We may find ourselves missing the big picture.

The truth is F. Scott Fitzgerald didn't have to consider himself a failure—he wasn't. With two successfully published novels, he was one of the best-paid writers of his time, and his work had inspired others who would go on to great fame and fortune, including Ernest Hemingway. As tragic a figure as he may be, what made Fitzgerald great was not his tragedy but his stubbornness. He did his best work when tapping into the tenacity that made him face the blank page after countless rejections. But when the barbs of critics wounded him, that same stubbornness worked against him, leading to an early end to his career. Grit may not have been able to save Fitzgerald's life, but it could have kept him creating.

STUBBORN BUT FLEXIBLE

In 1994, a thirty-year-old Princeton graduate and Wall Street success story made a bold career change after coming across a startling statistic. A new network called the World Wide Web was growing at 2300 percent per year. Did it mean anything? Many were shrugging, but the relatively young Jeff Bezos saw an opportunity. Within forty-eight hours of reading that statistic, he was on his way to creating what would become Amazon.com.

The idea of Amazon wasn't well received at first. "What's the Internet?" his father asked. Back in 1994, there was no way to know if the venture would be profitable or just a peculiar outlet for a soon-to-be Starving Artist. But Jeff started the company with a motto that defines its operations today: *We are stubborn on vision. We are flexible on details.*

For a business-minded creative, this means being ferociously entrepreneurial, even within a corporate environment. The company's 150,000 employees approach their jobs according to Amazon's fourteen leadership principles that grant them ownership of and responsibility for innovation and creativity. As a group, they have embraced Jeff's ethos that an entrepreneur must get comfortable with being misunderstood, which must be a great comfort every time they try something new.

Amazon has also failed miserably at times. They spent millions on a sixteen-month television advertising campaign that demonstrated dismal returns on investment. They tried online auctions and couldn't hold their own against eBay. Some would even call Amazon Prime a failure because it doesn't recoup its costs, but Bezos reframes that as a marketing expense. In the end, failures at Amazon are just details, Bezos would say, and they're flexible on those.

"If you think that's a big failure," he once said of the Fire Phone, "we're working on much bigger failures right now. And I am not kidding . . . Every single important thing that we have done has taken a lot of risk taking, perseverance, guts, and some of them have worked out; most of them have not."

When he was eighteen, Bezos was quoted as saying he wanted to build hotels, amusement parks, and colonies for two million people—all in outer space. Turns out, he's always been interested in space travel. He didn't know how he'd get there, only that it would take a creative mind to figure it out. He had vision, but the details were still unclear.

When Amazon made him the fifth richest man in the world, the stubborn entrepreneur found a way and quietly began building Blue Origin in the background of his everyday responsibilities. The aerospace company was launched with the Latin motto *Gradatim Ferociter*, which describes not only how we might end up leaving the planet one day but also how we can all succeed as artists in the meantime: *step by step, ferociously.*

As an entrepreneur, Bezos is no stranger to criticism. He understands that it comes to almost all of us, as do hardship and failure—these are the guarantees of creative work. But what we do when those trials come determines our success far more than any circumstance. Starving Artists tend to be stubborn about all things. Imagine them slaving away in studios, pumping out piece after piece, growing angrier each time something doesn't succeed. We say the definition of insanity is doing the same thing over and over but expecting different results, and that's the Starving Artist mentality embodied. Stubborn to a fault.

Thriving Artists, however, are flexible on details but stubborn on vision. They do not take personally praises or criticism. They persevere so that they can keep doing their work. Realizing success is not up to them, their job is to continue creating. And if we want to follow in their footsteps, we must do the same, careful to not fixate on the details and harness our strategic stubbornness.

SAY YES

At the age of twenty-four, Zach Prichard was working at a record label just outside of Nashville, Tennessee. In high school he moved with his family from Pensacola, Florida, to Tennessee and stayed in the area to study music business at Middle Tennessee State University. He completed college by taking night classes and selling calendars at a mall kiosk during the day.

> STARVING ARTISTS ARE STUBBORN ABOUT ALL THINGS. THRIVING ARTISTS ARE STUBBORN ABOUT THE RIGHT THINGS.

In 2005, while still in school, he got a job working in the music business, which had been his dream. However, it turned out to be a nightmare. The work was mostly administrative, not creative as he had hoped, and soon he was unhappy with his job, wondering if there was something better waiting for him.

One day in September 2010, Zach opened a mass e-mail from his favorite author, who was struggling to turn his bestselling spiritual memoir into a feature film. In the e-mail, the author, Donald Miller, said the project was running out of money and on the verge of failure. An investor had pulled out, and if he couldn't come up with additional funding, Miller would have to pull the plug on the film adaptation of *Blue Like Jazz*.

Staring at the computer screen in front of him and feeling stuck in his dead-end job, Zach decided to do something about his situation. He called a friend, and together they came up with an idea to do a Kickstarter fund-raiser to raise the extra $100,000 needed to finish the film. They were going to do it in a month, and all they needed was the approval of a *New York Times* bestselling author. They e-mailed Miller with their proposal: they would create a website, run a social media campaign, and create collateral to promote the campaign, which they called "Save Blue Like Jazz."

Within a couple of hours, the author had responded, asking for more information.

That night, Zach read the e-mail but was too nervous to respond. He tossed and turned for the better part of an hour before finally turning to his wife, Tracie, to tell her his mind just wouldn't stop racing. She said, "I think you need to go work on this *now*."

Everything sensible was telling Zach to go to bed, but something in him just wouldn't let it go. Just before midnight, he and his friend met for a late-night session of white-boarding, strategizing, and planning. They put it all together in a proposal letter they e-mailed to Donald Miller just a few minutes before sunrise. The e-mail included everything they would do to try to save the

film project and how they would do it. They had never done anything like this, never worked with bestselling authors or large-scale
crowd-funding campaigns, and here they were, laying it all out. It
seemed like a long shot, but it was just the kind of stubbornness that
another artist might admire.

Until this point, the most successful crowd-funding campaign
had raised approximately $80,000, and their plan was to break that
record—without having any experience whatsoever. It was stubborn
work, based on the belief that they could do this despite all the odds,
but it was also the kind of outlet Zach had been craving for some
time. He didn't think much about that at five o'clock in the morning when he put the finishing touches on their plan and sent off the
e-mail. He took a quick nap, then showered and went to work, a
strange sense of invigoration following him for the rest of the day.

Before the end of the day, Zach received a reply from Miller
saying he was in. And just like that, the campaign was born. In the
next thirty days, Zach and his friend would work harder than they'd
ever worked before. What they lacked in experience, they made
up for in tenacity, working early mornings, nights, and weekends.
Whenever they weren't at their full-time jobs, they spent their time
blogging and posting on social media about the campaign. They
also did media interviews and answered e-mails from all over the
world. "It felt like a presidential campaign," Zach recalled.

All that hard work paid off with 4,495 financial backers pledg-
ing $345,992, helping to bring the project to life. "We broke all
the records that day," Zach said. "Biggest project on Kickstarter.
Highest crowd-funded movie. Project of the year."

Soon after the success of the campaign, Zach was offered
another job on the set of the film. The director asked him to take
behind-the-scenes photos of the movie-making process for the fans

who had helped fund the picture. Zach was given a camera he didn't know how to use, and once again, he jumped into a job he was less than qualified to do. Through stubborn trial and error, he figured out this new medium, which evolved into other opportunities. He continued to be involved in the project, eventually getting to do additional film work.

After the shooting of the movie, Zach and his friend who ran the Kickstarter campaign started a film production company called Rhetorik. For years, they partnered together on commercials, music videos, and other multimedia projects before finally parting ways and forming separate companies. The last time I spoke to Zach, he was finishing up a "30 for 30" ESPN documentary on the tragic but heroic death of NFL star Joe Delaney. Now he is an in-demand film editor.

I asked Zach if he wondered what would have happened had he gone to bed that night instead of getting up, going to his friend's house, and sending that e-mail. Would he have still gotten the gig? "Absolutely not," he told me. "That was a once-in-a-lifetime opportunity, and we both knew it."

We are told artists are stubborn, and they certainly can be. But this isn't always a bad thing. Stubbornness can be an essential ingredient in making a living off your art. When you harness your strategic stubbornness, you give the world a reason to believe in your work.

WHEN TO QUIT

Michelangelo was thirty years old when he began working on a tomb for Pope Julius II in February 1505. Three stories tall, with forty life-size figures and other ornaments, it was going to be a sight to behold. The artist's dreams for the piece were so grandiose that he confessed there was "a madness that came over me."

WHEN YOU HARNESS YOUR STRATEGIC STUBBORNNESS, YOU GIVE THE WORLD A REASON TO BELIEVE IN YOUR WORK.

But when the pope began to lose interest in the project, Michelangelo grew angry. Unable to get the pope's attention for a couple of months in 1506, he fled Rome without the pope's permission. This did not please the papacy, and Michelangelo, who was now an outlaw, had to take refuge under the Florentine governor's protection.

Pope Julius summoned the defiant artist, and the two worked out their disagreements, agreeing to continue the project. The artist apologized to the pope and sculpted a statue of him, likely as a form of penance. At the heart of Michelangelo's sudden departure was a demand for respect—one of the first times in history that an artist set the terms of his work. "Michelangelo and Julius were redefining the relations between artist and patron," wrote historian William Wallace.

Michelangelo's correspondence in 1506 and 1507 reads like that of a tired and overburdened artist. "I live in great discomfort and fatigue," he wrote to his brother in November 1507. "I do little other than work day and night, and it has been a hard and difficult labor." The difference between Michelangelo and F. Scott Fitzgerald is that he didn't end his letter there. Instead, he summoned his stubbornness, channeled it into grit, and concluded, "It is enough that I have brought it to completion."

In the spring of 1508, Julius reassigned Michelangelo from the tomb to the painting of the Sistine Chapel ceiling. That might have been the end of the tomb, but refusing again to give up, Michelangelo scaled the tomb's design down to a more manageable size and returned to it repeatedly until it was completed in 1545, forty years after he had started it. He could have walked away a dozen times, but he didn't—that's the grit of a real artist. Michelangelo might have been difficult to work with, he might even have defied popes and other powerful patrons, but he was stubborn as a donkey, and that's why he completed so many great works. Stubbornness was a tool he learned to use for the benefit of his art.

We are used to thinking of stubbornness as something to be avoided. It often takes the shape of impulsive behavior or of not filtering our own thoughts, then later we are forced to face the consequences of our actions. But it can also be crucial to the success of an artist. Steve Jobs's "reality distortion field" is a notable example of this, as demonstrated by a story from Andy Herzfeld, who had just joined the Apple team in 1981. Andy recalls arguing with coworker Bud Tribble on the deadline to release the original Macintosh software in ten months. "That's impossible," Andy said, knowing how many details had to fall exactly in line, but such things hardly mattered to the stubborn CEO. "In [Jobs's] presence, reality is malleable," Bud told Andy. "He can convince anyone of practically anything. It wears off when he's not around, but it makes it hard to have realistic schedules."

One kind of stubbornness can push a person away and lead to their demise, as was the case with Fitzgerald's inability to persevere and getting lost in the failure of his work. Michelangelo, on the other hand, learned to channel his stubbornness into grit, so that even though the Julius tomb was initially canceled, he continued reviving the project for the rest of his life, eventually completing it at the age of seventy.

Most people tend to make use of only a small amount of their resources, whereas, to quote Angela Duckworth, "a few exceptional individuals push themselves to their limits." This is grit in action, and the effect is a heightened level of focus and intensity on the work. What makes you stubborn in one area of life can make you successful in another, if you learn to harness the ability.

For many years, Michelangelo's stubbornness was a liability, but as he matured, it became an asset, something he used for the benefit of his work instead of his ego. Stubbornness gets in the way when it's about you—your fame, your reputation, your success—but it becomes a tool when used to further your work.

STUBBORN ENOUGH TO SUCCEED

Starting in February 1943, three years after F. Scott Fitzgerald's death, the Council on Books in Wartime capitalized on the innovation of paperback printing and sent 150,000 copies of *The Great Gatsby* to soldiers overseas. After being circulated during World War II, the novel became popular as many soldiers returned home with the story imprinted on their minds.

In the 1950s, due in part to its brevity, *Gatsby* was introduced to high school English curriculums, causing even wider success. By 1960, the book was selling fifty thousand copies per year, a trend that continues today and has only been boosted by the appearance and reappearance of the story on movie screens. To date, the novel has sold more than twenty-five million copies.

Ironically, Fitzgerald's book endured even when he did not. But what might have happened to the author if he hadn't given up so soon? What if he'd had more grit, been a little more tenacious, and harnessed his stubbornness? Had he endured just a few more years, he may very well have seen *Gatsby* become the bestseller it is today. And what other works might he have given us, if he'd found a way to turn his stubbornness into tenacity?

Sometimes, when we see a creative person succeed, we dismiss his breakthrough as luck or the result of pure talent, but neither explanation is accurate. What often allows great work to get the attention it deserves is not a matter of only talent or luck but a matter of the will. Can you stick around long enough to see your work succeed? Do you have enough grit to take a few critical hits and keep going? Or will you get discouraged at the first sign of failure? Zach Prichard had no experience running a crowd-funding campaign, much less doing media work. But what he did have was stubbornness, and he could figure out the rest. The result was the largest crowd-funding campaign Kickstarter had ever seen.

How many other people would have stayed up all night on a whim to earn just the *chance* to fund-raise for a project that had little hope of succeeding? Let's not forget Zach wasn't getting paid to do any of this. It was a volunteer opportunity that would take up his nights and weekends for months while he still had to hold down a day job. Fortunately, he had the tenacity to not only start such an endeavor but to see it through. He had the vision and wasn't distracted by the details, so when he saw his chance to succeed, he took it.

But let's not misinterpret what happened here: talent did not do this; tenacity did. If you want to see your work succeed, you must be stubborn. You must be willing to keep going, even in the face of adversity. On the surface, stubbornness may look like a liability, but in creative work, it can be an asset. A little tenacity can fuel our pursuit of excellence, giving us the grit we need to create lasting work.

We must be wary, however, to not let our need for greatness hijack the work itself. Flexible on details, but stubborn on vision, as Jeff Bezos would say. Yes, this work takes some stubbornness, but that should be nothing new for an artist.

The question is, are you stubborn enough to succeed?

ARE YOU

STUBBORN

ENOUGH TO SUCCEED?

Part 2

MARKET

ONCE WE HAVE MASTERED OUR MIND-SETS, WE MUST TACKLE THE market. Here, we cross the threshold from being creative to doing creative work. This is the place where we become professionals and learn how this works in the real world. This is where we network and advertise our talents to the masses. And if we do this well, people will not just pay attention, they will also pay us.

Chapter 5

Cultivate Patrons

> The Starving Artist waits to be noticed.
> The Thriving Artist cultivates patrons.

*If there hadn't been a Sam Phillips, I might
still be working in a cotton field.*
—Johnny Cash

IN SEPTEMBER 1948, THE PRESLEY FAMILY MOVED FROM TUPELO,
Mississippi, to Memphis, Tennessee, in search of work. They lived
in public housing and struggled to make ends meet. At night, their
only son would sit outside in the courtyard, inexpertly playing the
guitar and singing the blues—dreaming of another life. Around
that same time, another man in Memphis had a dream of his own.

At 706 Union Avenue, Sam Phillips's Sun Studio had a reputation for signing no-name musicians. Their slogan was: "We record
anything, anywhere, any time." The fledgling studio had already
seen the likes of B. B. King, Howlin' Wolf, and Ike Turner, but
Phillips's vision for bringing black music to a white audience was
still a distant reality. He needed the right voice, which so far had
eluded him.

One day in 1954, a nineteen-year-old truck driver entered

Phillips's studio. When the music producer wasn't discovering new talent, he charged for his recording services at a rate of four dollars per record. Many musicians in Memphis were all too eager to pay, including the young man who entered the studio that day to cut a record for his mother. After the first visit, he would return a few months later to record another for himself—a "personal" record, he called it. The young musician continued stopping by the studio to say hello. Phillips's assistant Marion Keisker was especially taken with the boy, later remembering him as being perpetually nervous and stammering over his words. The most the producer would give him, however, was that he was "an interesting singer" and that they might call on him sometime.

Months later, the guitarist Scotty Moore was looking for a singer to join his band and asked Phillips for any recommendations. When the producer said he didn't have any, Marion mentioned the young man from Mississippi. What was his name—*Elvis*? They decided to bring him back into the studio.

From the outset, no one shared Marion's enthusiasm. The boy could sing well enough but neither Phillips nor Moore heard anything special. Three hours into the audition, they took a break, having played through several songs with no luck. When the two men compared their notes, both concluded the young singer was not their guy.

During the break, Elvis picked up a guitar and began to play. The clumsy strumming pattern created a staccato sound that served as his own rhythm section, and he started to sing. Like an old, almost forgotten memory, the song came to him: "That's All Right Mama" by Arthur Crudup. Jumping around the room, Elvis belted out the words to the blues tune, his energy contagious, and soon the guitarist and bassist were joining him. An audition that only moments before had been leading to rejection was now being transformed into something powerful. Phillips, who was cutting tape in the sound room, stopped what he was doing to listen, then interrupted the trio.

"What are you doing?" he asked.

"We don't know," they answered.

"Well, back up," he responded. "Try to find a place to start, and do it again."

It took several takes to simplify the sound, but by the end of the night, the three musicians had a record. More important than that, the young guitar-playing truck driver had someone who finally believed in him. The next day, Sam Phillips took the single to local radio station WHBQ, where his friend Dewey Phillips (no relation) worked as a disc jockey. Dewey shared Sam's love for the blues and loved breaking in new musicians to the Memphis scene. He listened to the new cut and loved it, putting the record on the air that night. "That's All Right Mama" played at least four more times before dawn, with people requesting it daily after that.

The three musicians started touring with Sam Phillips as their manager. Within two years, Elvis Presley would become a household name, playing for crowds of tens of thousands, appearing on television, starring in films, and reaching an audience of millions. In an unbelievably short amount of time, the young man's dreams had come true. The first song he officially recorded, which he didn't even write, made him a star. The producer who first rejected him helped him get a record deal. And the world that was once indifferent to him now embraced him like they had never before.

It's your typical tale of overnight success, the kind we tell young artists who are waiting to be discovered. Just keep practicing, we say, and maybe you'll catch your lucky break someday. But that's the wrong advice, because you don't just need practice. You also need a patron.

THE RULE OF THE PATRON

In creative work, quality is subjective. How do you determine if a painting is good or bad? What makes a song beautiful? Objectively speaking, these things are hard to measure. What we need, then, are authorities on art. We need someone to tell us Bob Dylan is a genius and Vincent van Gogh was ahead of his time. Otherwise, we are left to make such determinations on our own, and we are often mistaken about who ends up being a genius.

> ## YOU DON'T JUST NEED PRACTICE.
> ## YOU ALSO NEED A PATRON.

We tend to trust the opinions of experts over those of others, sometimes even our own; and if we ignore this phenomenon, we do so at our own peril. Those of us who aren't connoisseurs don't want to spend the time figuring out what kind of music to listen to or which books to read. Most of us get our sense of what's good from a special group of connoisseurs, those superfans whom researcher Elizabeth Currid calls "tastemakers." These influencers are the ones who can make or break a career, depending on whether they vouch for you. We need these people to not only help us decide what good art is but also to help us succeed as artists ourselves.

This is nothing new, of course; it is an old idea, dating back even before the Renaissance, when patrons and artists helped usher important work into the world. Creative work of all kinds has always needed generous benefactors to help it succeed, and if you aspire to share your art with the world, you are going to need one too.

Behind many creative geniuses, there is often an invisible

influencer—a patron—making it all happen. These people lend their resources and influence to help creative talents succeed, introducing them to opportunities they would not encounter otherwise. This is the Rule of the Patron, which states that before you reach an audience of many, you must first reach an audience of one. Every artist needs a patron. Without one, your success becomes exponentially more difficult; with one, it becomes not only possible but probable.

BEFORE YOU REACH AN AUDIENCE OF MANY, YOU MUST FIRST REACH AN AUDIENCE OF ONE.

Starving Artists disdain the need for patrons. It feels disempowering, even beneath them. On the other hand, Thriving Artists respect the Rule of the Patron and use it to their advantage. All creative workers need influencers who will vouch for them to an audience who doesn't know them yet. But it is not enough to meet a patron; you must cultivate one. This was what Elvis Presley learned when he met Sam Phillips. Before meeting Sam, Elvis was just a kid who dressed funny and could sing well enough, but after winning the music producer over, Elvis became an international celebrity. The point at which everything changed, however, was not the first time he met Sam. It was the night he convinced the producer to believe in him.

If you are going to create work that matters, you are going to need an advocate—a person who sees your potential and believes in your work. This isn't just about money. You need someone to give you a chance, maybe even connect you to the right people. The publisher who pays an author's book advance is a patron. The venture capitalist who funds a start-up in Silicon Valley is one too. But so is the church who gives a minister a salary or the donors who support nonprofit organizations around the world. Patrons do not just make the arts possible; they make the world we inhabit—and so often take for granted—possible.

These are the people history forgets, the ones who don't always make it into textbooks. And one of the worst mistakes we could make is failing to recognize their existence or importance. Our job, then, isn't to wait for patrons to come to us but to find and cultivate these relationships, wherever they may be.

Closer than You Think

Years after Elvis's death, Sam Phillips lamented in an interview that his style of discovering artists didn't work anymore. Producers, he said, are not spending countless hours each week in bars, waiting to find that hot, new talent. So, where are today's patrons? How do we find these tastemakers whose influence will help us succeed? Do they even exist anymore? Of course, they do. You don't get art without money; and you don't get an artist without a patron. But these people are closer than we think. In the New Renaissance, patrons are not some elite class of influencers. They are all around us.

My first year out of college I traveled across North America playing music with a band. As the group's leader, I oversaw setting up gigs ahead of time, coordinating with event planners and hosts, and making sure everyone arrived at the show on time. This was not the glorious experience I imagined when dreaming of "life on the road"—it was a lot of hard work, long days, and cold casseroles.

But one factor made the work possible: the fact that we didn't have to do it alone. Moving from city to city, our band would play shows in exchange for donations and meals; we were always at the mercy of other people's generosity. No matter where we went, we met someone who would make sure we found a good meal, warm bed, and sometimes even a hot shower. For a year, we lived off the good nature of other people, staying in their homes and eating their food, getting to make our art.

Everything we did that year cost something: the gasoline for the van, the meals on the road, the occasional night in a hotel when we couldn't find a host home. It all had to be paid for by someone. My six bandmates and I didn't have to worry about any of that, though, because there were people concerned about those things *for* us. They paid our bills and took care of our expenses; they hosted events for us and took us into their homes. They were the ones who fed us and took care of us, going out of their way to help however they could—all so that we could focus on our music.

These people were our patrons. However, they were not wealthy connoisseurs or influential leaders. They were ordinary people who used their resources to help our art thrive. Wherever we went, they were there. Certainly, there can be value in connecting with a famous tastemaker, but sometimes, the patron you need is the one who is right in front of you.

These people may be hard to recognize, but help is always available to those willing to look. In the case of Elvis, Sam Phillips was just down the road from him. For my band, our patrons were the people we met at each show. All around us there are patrons, people willing to help our work succeed. But it is our job to recognize them and prove ourselves worthy of their investment.

BE TEACHABLE

When Michelangelo was still an apprentice under Domenico Ghirlandaio, he was working outside one day, finishing up a new sculpture. A well-dressed man approached the young artist to watch him carve the mask of a fawn and inquired about the statue. When Michelangelo said it was meant to be an antique fawn, the guest suggested that if it were an old fawn, it should have some teeth missing. Then, the mysterious man walked away. He returned the next day and saw some teeth had been knocked out of the fawn's mouth.

SOMETIMES, THE PATRON YOU NEED IS THE ONE WHO IS RIGHT IN FRONT OF YOU.

The man was none other than Lorenzo de Medici, the wealthiest man in Florence and a great patron of the arts. Shortly after meeting Michelangelo, Lorenzo summoned the teenage artist to come work in his royal palace. The rest of the boy's youth was spent surrounded by art and influence beyond his wildest dreams—all because he had first reached an audience of one. This is the Rule of the Patron in action. You can't just ask for a handout; you must demonstrate both competency in your craft and a willingness to learn. Influencers love to inspire and invest in others, so make it easy on them. When the Starving Artist waits to be noticed, the Thriving Artist finds a patron and shows that her work is worth investing in.

When I met Michael Hyatt, the CEO of a large publishing company at the time, I experienced this firsthand. We met at the local Starbucks in Franklin, Tennessee, the town we both happened to live in at the time, at four o'clock in the afternoon on an unusually warm and sunny day in November. For years I had followed his work, knowing he had wisdom that would benefit me as a young writer. I also knew he was busy, so I reached out with a sample of my writing and a request to meet whenever was convenient for him.

We met for about an hour, seated by the window, sipping our black coffees. For most of the time, he sprung question after question on me, which I was not ready for. It was an unexpected act of generosity but one that I almost wasted by being unprepared. After the meeting, I followed up with an e-mail thanking him for his time and sharing how I was already putting his advice to use. Over time, we maintained a regular correspondence, and he continued to show interest in my writing.

Because of Michael's connections in publishing, my career was put on a fast track. He started introducing me to influential people and championing my work wherever he could. At the time, I couldn't believe my good fortune. An unlikely connection grew into a friendship that led to exponential growth for me. At one point he shared several of my blog posts with his followers, and I sent him a message. Overwhelmed by his generosity, I said, "You don't have to keep doing this. You can stop now."

"Jeff," he said, "I don't know what you're talking about. I share your stuff because it's good, and I like it."

Later when I pressed him for why he said yes to our initial coffee meeting, he told me it was because he had read my writing and liked it. He told me what made it easy for him to say yes was the convenience factor (we lived in the same town), the potential I had (I was already doing the work), and a lack of neediness on my part (I just wanted to meet him for coffee). Turns out, I wasn't the first person he had done this for, and since meeting him I haven't been the last.

Influencers want to help people. They want to invest in others.

They just need to know that you're worth their time, which means your abilities need to be obvious. Your job, then, is to get to work, because the best way to win over a patron is to show them your potential, and the best demonstration of your ability is the work itself. This doesn't mean you must be suddenly amazing—most artists in need of a patron are not. But it does mean that you should be working and, more importantly, be willing to learn.

When we allow ourselves to be teachable, we attract those who would influence us and help our work spread. After all, it was not Michelangelo who went to Lorenzo, but Lorenzo who came to him. It was the artist's willingness to learn that endeared the young man to his patron, and it will be that same spirit that earns you one, as well.

USE YOUR DAY JOB

There are, of course, different kinds of patrons, and not all of us will be so lucky as to have a wealthy investor show up in our studios as was the case for Michelangelo. But remember that patrons are all around us, even sometimes in our day jobs. That's what Kabir Sehgal found when he used his career in investment banking to launch a career in art.

Growing up in Atlanta, Georgia, Kabir wanted to do everything from music to business to politics. After college, he was hired by JP Morgan and quickly rose through the ranks. During his eight years there, he wrote five books, produced several Grammy award-winning albums, and served in the US Navy Reserve—all while being a significant revenue producer at his job. How did he do it? He used his day job as a kind of patron for the art he wanted to create. Kabir has always considered himself a creative person, but he never assumed he had to suffer for his art. Unlike some, he did not quit his job and leap out into the unknown. Instead, he did what many of us may have to do if we want our creative work to survive. He used his current scenario and surroundings as a means to an end, as opposed to an impediment to his goals.

In the Renaissance, patrons were not benefactors who lavishly gave of their wealth to artists without any say over what they wanted the artists to create. In most cases, they gave commissions with specifications about what they wanted made and how it should be done. In other words, even if you had a patron, you still had a boss. So why not use your current boss and start seeing this person as a patron of your work, even if they don't see themselves that way? In the New Renaissance, these opportunities are myriad, and if you follow the rules of the Thriving Artist, you can give yourself time and space to create the work you want.

Working in banking, as you can imagine, requires its own skill set—skills very different from, say, writing. Kabir wanted to write badly enough, however, that he was willing to figure out a way to write, even with a busy and demanding schedule. "The compliance department taught me how to write books," he said, meaning he used the mundane tasks of his job to help him practice writing. This was how he wrote the first of five books while working on Wall Street.

This approach of using a day job allows the artist greater flexibility and freedom to do better work without needing to make a living off it. Kabir knew art costs money, and there was no guarantee his creative work would generate enough money for him to live, so he used his day job to fund his art and was paid to practice his craft in the meantime. Kabir didn't try to opt out of the system, claiming he didn't need to make money. Instead, he embraced the reality that without income, an artist can't create, and then he used his circumstances to his benefit.

While working in finance, Kabir was required to write daily memos to investors. These were typically boring updates filled with industry jargon, but he used this as a chance to sharpen his skills, writing them in the form of haikus. This kept him creative in a job that could have sapped his creativity and made him stand out among his peers at work. That is an interesting by-product to this strategy: sometimes using your day job can result not only in getting paid to create but also in doing your day job better.

Many people aspire to do creative work but worry they won't have enough freedom or time to do it. They mistakenly believe they should quit their jobs to start writing that novel or to tour full time with the band. And in some cases, this may be true. But Kabir's story confounds such stereotypes. He used his situation to be creative, and it worked—better, perhaps, than quitting his job would have. And Kabir is not an anomaly. According to him, there are many artists and creative types who end up on Wall Street. Few, however, can stay there with their creativity intact.

Wall Street, he wrote in an article for CNBC, "is where creativity goes to die." Yet clearly, in his case, that was not true. People end up in that very competitive world of banking because they are motivated and smart and often find themselves in lucrative careers before they know what their passions are. Many people leave Wall Street to chase their passions once they realize what they really want in life. This was the crossroads where Kabir found himself when he realized he wanted to write. What made him different from the rest of the burnouts, though, was that he was constantly cultivating patrons.

What do you do when you find yourself in a position that is less than ideal? Do you quit your job and try to strike out on your own? Not at all. You look around for the closest patron, even if that means your day job. "Follow your curiosities and get a paycheck," Kabir told me. "Don't focus so much on the job, but on the ideals and the goals." Any job can be a means to making your art, if you have the right perspective. Employers become patrons when we begin to see them not as obstacles to the work we want to do but as a way of funding it.

PURSUING PATRONS

Originally from Florence, Alabama, Sam Phillips grew up watching black people and white people work the fields together. This left an indelible impression on him. After moving to Memphis, Tennessee, which was much more segregated, he wanted to record the kind of music he grew up with in hopes that it would bring people together. But he struggled with getting the music he loved to the masses. What he needed was an evangelist.

Enter Elvis.

Elvis Presley knocked on Sam Phillips's door, looking for someone to believe in him, but the music producer had also been waiting. And when he met a white boy who could sing black music the way it needed to be sung, he knew he had found something special. The partnership that resulted from this meeting changed music forever.

Typically, when we talk about creative success, we tend to place a lot of emphasis on the genius of the artist. This, we think, is what makes a musician like Elvis a rock star. But without a patron, without someone to vouch for the genius, most creative work will not spread very far. Creative work is a team effort—a duo of artist and patron, singer and producer, actor and manager. One is the talent and the other the advocate. Yes, artists need patrons, but what we sometimes miss is that patrons also need artists.

▲ YES, ARTISTS NEED PATRONS, BUT ▲ PATRONS ALSO NEED ARTISTS.

So how do we seek out the influencers and tastemakers who are all around us? We begin by finding the people who are already investing in others, who have wisdom and experience, and reach out to them. Finding a patron is a lot like finding a master: we put ourselves in the place where opportunity happens, making sure we have developed our craft so that we do not waste the person's time. When we knock on their doors, we need to be ready to receive what they have to offer. Most likely, we will not find these patrons far off. Often, they are in our own backyards, down the street, or around the corner. Sometimes they are even in our day jobs. Other times they are the relationships we may be neglecting, the loose ties with friends and acquaintances that could lead to a breakthrough. We just need to recognize them.

This begins by acknowledging the age in which we live. Today we don't have to wait to be noticed. This is a time when it's possible to make your own breaks and set yourself up for success—if you are willing to do the work. Share your competency with those who can help your work spread. Look for opportunity instead of waiting for it. Allow yourself to be taught and molded by those who come, and you will find your patron.

But let's be clear about something. You can't succeed alone. We all need someone to invest in our work. Without a Sam Phillips, we don't get an Elvis Presley. We also don't get a Jerry Lee Lewis or a Howlin' Wolf. As Johnny Cash once said, "If there hadn't been a Sam Phillips, I might still be working in a cotton field." It was the music producer's connections—the network he had spent years building with radio DJs, promoters, and musicians—that made Elvis and so many others into stars.

Without a patron, you're rolling the dice, hoping for the best—and the world is unkind to such gambles. The night "That's All Right Mama" hit the airwaves, a young musician named Lee Denson was playing a show in Key West. When the song played on the radio, he couldn't believe what he was hearing. Was this the same Elvis Presley whom he had tried to teach guitar only a few years before, the same young man who could barely play a chord? And here was Denson, doing everything a young musician ought to be doing—touring and playing shows, paying his dues—and it wasn't working. Of course it wasn't working. Denson didn't have a Sam Phillips, and when it comes to creative success, that's everything.

Chapter 6

Go Join a Scene

> The Starving Artist believes he
> can be creative anywhere.
> The Thriving Artist goes where creative
> work is already happening.

If you want to be creative, go where your questions lead you.
—Louis L'Amour

WHEN A YOUNG PARAMEDIC RETURNED HOME AFTER SERVING WITH the Red Cross in World War I, he had little idea where life would take him next. At nineteen years old, recuperating from the wounds of a mortar blast and a broken heart, his prospects were limited. On the Italian front, he had fallen in love with a nurse who had stopped answering his letters and run off with another man. Soon these experiences would serve as the foundation for a narrative that would transform him into one of the world's most famous authors, but at the moment, Ernest Hemingway was just another direction-less kid.

It didn't take long to realize Oak Park, Illinois, was not where Hemingway wanted to be. At the suggestion of a friend, he took a job at the *Toronto Star*, working as a journalist. A year later, he moved back to Chicago, where he fell in love with a young woman named Hadley Richardson. The two married and began making plans to relocate to Europe. Around that time, Hemingway met novelist Sherwood Anderson who told him to move to Paris because it was where the most interesting people in the world lived.

In Paris, Hemingway could work on his writing with his foreign correspondence work paying the bills. The couple could live modestly and still be able to travel. For a young, restless couple, it sounded like a dream. Not long after their wedding, the young writer and his new wife packed up their belongings, boarded a ship, and made their way to a new life.

When the young couple arrived in the Latin Quarter, the Hemingways found a small community of intellectuals and expatriates who were not unlike themselves. Through letters of introduction from Sherwood Anderson, they met many soon-to-be-famous authors and artists who would become some of their closest friends.

Living on the Left Bank, Hemingway met the influences who would shape his work and transform him into "Papa," the larger-than-life figure who would go on to define the literary style of a generation. But at the time, these acquaintances were simply their neighbors, fellow creatives trying to hack it out like everyone else.

Every morning, the young author would walk along the Seine River, watching the fishermen pull their catch out of the water, a reminder of childhood summers spent on Lake Michigan. Often he would stop at a café for a few hours and write, fictionalizing his youth while sipping a café crème or demi blonde. Everything he experienced became a part of him and his stories.

In his spare time, Hemingway would exchange boxing lessons for writing tips with Ezra Pound. At the Closerie de Lilas or Les

Deux Magots he sometimes spotted James Joyce or bumped into F. Scott Fitzgerald, who introduced him to editor Maxwell Perkins. In the evenings, he would stroll down to 27 Rue du Fleurus where Gertrude Stein lived, and listen to her lecture on the importance of buying paintings rather than clothes.

It all happened in Paris.

Hemingway spent the greater part of his twenties living in that community—what came to be called "The Lost Generation"—living on little, surrounded by brilliance. Life in that little Parisian neighborhood provided an invaluable education for an up-and-coming writer in the 1920s, and he used it all to fuel his writing. Later, he translated his experiences into *The Sun Also Rises*, a semiautobiographical novel that would earn him widespread fame. Before his time there, the young writer was certainly skilled but by no means famous, but when he returned to America seven years later, Ernest Hemingway had become a household name.

Considering all the people he met during his time there, it's hard to imagine such a transformation taking place had Hemingway not heeded Sherwood Anderson's advice. What *was* it about his time in Paris that made such a difference? Maybe it wasn't the time but the place.

THE RULE OF THE SCENE

One day college professor Richard Florida was walking across the campus of Carnegie Mellon University in Pittsburgh, Pennsylvania, when he saw a table surrounded by people. Several were wearing blue T-shirts with the name of an Austin-based software company. He asked if they were recruiting students. "No, absolutely not," they said. They had come to hang out for the day, all the way from Austin. *What a strange thing to do*, Professor Florida thought.

Later in the day, he heard that a student who had been a part of the crowd had just signed a contract with the company. It was the highest-paying deal any graduating student in the history of his department had ever received. When Florida asked the student, covered in tattoos and piercings, why he was going to a smaller city in the middle of Texas, a place that lacked many of the cultural amenities of Pittsburgh, the young man replied, "It's in *Austin!*" It was the city that ultimately clinched the deal for him.

What attracted the student to Austin was not a century's worth of industry, as Pittsburgh could boast, but a thriving music scene, cultural diversity, and a bustling nightlife. Despite offers from other tech firms in larger cities, the young man decided on a city known for its progressive politics and eclectic culture because he believed that was where he'd do his best work. This student is part of what Richard Florida calls the Creative Class, a growing group of professionals that are quickly becoming an important part of society. This growing group of creative workers now makes up a third of the labor force, working in a wide range of industries from technology to entertainment, journalism to finance, and manufacturing to the arts. And one of the most important issues for a member of the Creative Class is location.

Some places have an "it" factor. We see this in architecturally beautiful cities like Rome or Paris, which are full of amazing art and well-designed buildings. Other places serve as hotbeds for certain industries, such as the personal computer revolution launched in Silicon Valley. We intuitively grasp that certain locations are more attractive than others. This, of course, applies to creative work, as well, maybe even especially. "The most important factor in the success of your career," Richard Florida told me, "is where you decide to live."

This is the Rule of the Scene, which says that places and people shape the success of our work far more than we realize. Location is not irrelevant. Place matters. As social psychologist Mihaly Csikszentmihalyi wrote, "Creativity is more likely in places where new ideas require less effort to be perceived."

The Starving Artist thinks she can do her work anywhere, but the Thriving Artist understands that where we live and do our work affects the work itself.

As artists, we want to be where we feel understood. We want to live in places where our work and way of life are encouraged. When musician and author Patti Smith was asked why New York was an attractive place for creatives in the 1970s, she said, "It was cheap to live here, really cheap. There were so many of us, so many like minds." We go where there are others like us, and these scenes can help our work thrive. Such hotspots of creativity, when properly harnessed, can become powerful spurs to creative work.

In the early twentieth century, Paris was such a scene. It was inexpensive, tolerant toward unconventional lifestyles, and attractive to artists. So, it is 1921. What does a fledgling journalist who wants to be a serious writer do? He boards a ship and moves to Paris, joining that community of artists and expats living there. He embeds himself in the creative scene, befriending the leading literary minds of the time, and profits from the opportunities such a place affords. Without Paris, you do not get Hemingway; and without a scene, you do not get a creative genius.

SCENES BEGET NETWORKS

When Hank Willis Thomas enrolled in graduate school, he was trying to avoid getting a job. But when his cousin was murdered in 2000, he began using photography and visual art to process the experience. "Art was part of my mourning process," he said.

> ## WITHOUT A SCENE, YOU DO NOT GET A CREATIVE GENIUS.

His time at California College of the Arts became a kind of extended therapy, during which he threw himself into his creative work. When his studies ended in 2004, Hank thought it was time to get a "real" job, but in grad school he had stumbled upon a surprising lesson, which led to his eventual success as an artist.

"What grad school does," he explained, "is help you build a network."

As an art student, Hank had accidentally built something every artist needs, something so essential that without it, success is all but impossible. A network is more than a team of cheerleaders; it's a diverse group of individuals who offer a set of skills and resources that help each member succeed. After all, not every art student becomes an artist. Some become curators, community organizers, and patrons; others become collectors, dealers, and auction house owners. And nearly all become entrepreneurs of some sort, buying and selling in ways that contribute to the business of art. These are the people Hank Willis Thomas met in art school, and they are the ones who later became his network.

After graduation, Hank saw the careers of his friends take off and was surprised to see how those connections influenced the success of his work. He sold a piece of artwork—a black-and-white photograph of a group of college students holding a picture frame while others documented the event—to the son of the dean at the Tisch School of the Arts at New York University. That was his first sale as an artist. It happened as the result of a connection he'd made thanks to the scene he was a part of, a benefit of the network he'd grown.

Word of mouth spread and, to his surprise, soon Hank Willis Thomas was selling his art for a living. Those early successes were the building blocks of a career that over the years would blossom into a full-time living, making Hank a respected artist in New York City. Today his work has been featured in galleries and projects all over the country. He has a strong social media following, influencing tens of thousands of fans every day, much of it thanks to those people he met in art school. "All my great opportunities have come from friends," he said. "You really only need one or two good friends, because it's really about having someone who's going to advocate for you. That's the formula for success."

Thriving Artists do not succeed in a vacuum. They put themselves in the right places and avail themselves of the opportunities there. They don't try to create just anywhere—that would be foolish. After all, not all places are created equal, so Thriving Artists go where the magic is. But this takes more than moving to a new city. You have to join a scene, wherever you find one, and that means making connections with the people who will help your work succeed. In other words, you have to build a network.

Without a network, creative work does not succeed. Exposure to the right networks can accelerate your success like few things can. This flies in the face of what we typically expect an artist to do or say. "All my great opportunities have come from friends," Hank said. Great work does not come about through a single stroke of genius, but by the continual effort of a community. When the right people advocate for your work, your success becomes more likely. Being good is necessary, but it is not sufficient. Skill is a prerequisite for creative success, but talent is only part of the equation. The rest is network.

> ## GREAT WORK DOES NOT COME ABOUT THROUGH A SINGLE STROKE OF GENIUS, BUT BY THE CONTINUAL EFFORT OF A COMMUNITY.

A network is your insurance against anonymity. The greater access you have to influential people in your field, the further your work will spread. Of course, you have to be good, but being good is not enough. Skill gets you in front of the right people, but network magnifies your reach. Creative success, then, is contingent on your ability to connect well with those who can vouch for your work. It doesn't take a lot of people—just a few friends, as Hank said. You don't need an army, but you do need a network.

The exposure you gain from these relationships is invaluable. When no one is paying attention to your work, these connections can keep you from starving. No one succeeds alone, not even creative geniuses.

WHEN THEY REJECT YOU

During his early twenties, Vincent van Gogh moved from one job to the next, working first as an art dealer, then as a schoolteacher, and later as a missionary. Each transition was accompanied by a renewed but short-lived zeal. He seemed immature and reckless, and by all accounts was.

Then, at twenty-seven years old, Van Gogh taught himself a new set of skills. First he learned to draw, and then he learned to paint. With no formal training, the young artist tackled his craft, tirelessly creating an impressive body of work in a short amount of time. Unlike his previous professions, he did not quit this career. And today his works are some of the most valuable pieces of art on the planet.

When we think of Vincent van Gogh, we probably think of a lone genius—the maniac artist who cut off his ear, suffered for his art, and took his own life; the madman living in poverty and isolation. It's hard to imagine a more stereotypical picture of a Starving Artist. The problem, however, is this depiction is incomplete. Though Van Gogh likely had some sort of mental illness, it was not the madness that made his art succeed. It was his network.

Long before the world knew his name, Vincent van Gogh had a group of people who helped him become the artist we know him as today. Like every artist, he was not immune to the need for gatekeepers to validate his work. But how could he, a penniless and failed missionary, earn his place in the art scene?

When Vincent began his career as a painter, he had a vision for what he wanted to accomplish. His painting, however, was sloppy and imprecise, unpalatable to the mainstream art critics. He used too much paint and was reckless with his use of color and texture. The work was difficult to categorize; some thought it looked like child's play. Even his own mother criticized it. Who, then, could vouch for him?

It began with his younger brother Theo, a successful art dealer. Through letters, Theo's words kept Vincent going when life was hard, which was often. When Vincent decided to become an artist, Theo paid his bills, gave him a place to stay, and shared his work with others. He was his brother's patron and chief promoter.

Much of Van Gogh's career was filled with failure and rejection, but when he moved to Paris and met a group of painters whose work had been similarly rejected, he found his scene. These artists affirmed what Van Gogh was trying to do. In some ways, they understood it better than he did. They even had a name for it: *impressionism*. The French Impressionists could challenge and guide Van Gogh in the direction he was already headed, validating his work in the process. They became the network he needed, and that changed everything.

Once he became a member of their inner circle, Van Gogh gave back to that network, helping organize it into a more formal group and adopting the name "The Painters of the Petit Boulevard." Using his brother's connections, he helped display their works in galleries, and years later when the Impressionists were recognized for their artistic genius, his work was included among theirs.

The cruelty of life likely would have bankrupted Vincent van Gogh, were it not for the people who supported him. Life was not easy for him, but thanks to the support of his brother, he did not have to starve. The Impressionists encouraged and challenged him when others were prone to reject him.

When he died at the young age of thirty-seven, Van Gogh had painted thousands of canvases, the equivalent of a lifetime of work for many artists. Only months after his death, his brother Theo died, too, leaving his wife, Johanna, with a house full of paintings. Thanks to her husband's connections and her own network, she could sell off much of the artwork and help it get the attention it deserved.

A network of people validated Van Gogh's work and championed it long after he was gone. And it is to this network, not the efforts of a solitary artist, that we should be grateful.

This is the way creative work spreads: not through the efforts of a lone genius, but through a network. Remember, it was not an official group of gatekeepers who validated Van Gogh's art. It was a ragtag band of misfits with one thing in common—rejection—and that can be a powerful motivator. It wasn't that the Impressionists disregarded the power of networks. That would have meant career suicide. They simply redirected their efforts to create a new network, which raises an important question: What do you do when the network you want doesn't want you?

When you're playing a game you can't seem to win, sometimes the best thing to do is not try harder. None of us want to spend our lives playing by someone else's rules. When the game is unfair, change the game you're playing. Move to another city, create a new art form, get a different network. If the group you want to be a part of doesn't want you, then create your own.

This is what the Impressionists did when the gatekeepers of art in the nineteenth century rejected them. They opened their own gallery and invited people to it; and a century later, people remember them, not those who rejected them. And when a young misunderstood Dutchman joined that scene in Paris, he finally had a group of people who understood and validated his work.

Unlikely Genius Clusters

The Rule of the Scene shows us that not all places are created equal, and when we find the right scene, a network often follows. But these "scenes" are all around us. For one artist, it might be New Orleans, and for another, it's New York City. When we find the right place, however, we must dive in deep and become a part of the scene. And if we miss this opportunity, we miss a lot. Often, though, these scenes are not where we expect.

As travel writer Eric Weiner has explained, "Genius is a place, not a person." Weiner explored some of the most creative places on earth, such as Florence, Silicon Valley, and Paris, wondering what made these places such hotbeds of creativity. One surprising discovery was that most of these were unlikely places. Nobody could have predicted their contributions to the world—the Italian Renaissance, the birth of the personal computer, or even modern art. These creations were surprises to the outside world, and that's good news for all of us, because it means that what makes a place innovative and interesting is not some inherent quality. It means, maybe, that anywhere can be a genius cluster, if we understand how to use our surroundings.

"GENIUS IS A PLACE, NOT A PERSON."
—ERIC WEINER

In the mid-1970s, after traveling across the country in a van, Tracy Weisel moved to Jerome, Arizona, with his girlfriend Carol. In the spirit of experimentation and freedom that defined the decade, the couple was moving in hopes of getting away from the hustle and bustle of city life. In Jerome, Tracy made twenty dollars a day selling macramé necklaces and bracelets with clay beads. He and Carol kept their expenses low, living humbly off the sales of their art, and slowly began to build a life for themselves.

It took seven years to build a place of his own, from money earned by selling his pottery. For at least two years he set up his stand and potter's wheel on the sidewalk in front of his bulding site. His studio was the first new building in Jerome since the 1950s. "I wanted to build my own place because I got tired of landlords," he said. "So I bought my own property." When other artists began moving to Jerome due to the low cost of living, their artwork began attracting tourists. It's been thirty years since then, and thanks to the support of those tourists, Tracy has been able to make a living off his art ever since.

Today you can find him in his shop, blowing glass and entertaining audiences with stories and facts about his craft. He makes "normal things": a hummingbird feeder, wine glasses, whatever he thinks might sell. He does not consider his work "high art" by any means, but it's creative and fun and allows him to live the kind of life he wants. "To me," he told me over the phone one morning, "that's the fun of it: making a good, simple product."

Because of the support of a small town in Arizona, Tracy Weisel succeeded as an artist in ways that would not have been possible in other places. Most of the retail property in Jerome is owned by the historical society. The property never goes up for sale, so rent prices don't often rise. Compared to a place like Sedona, rent in Jerome is cheap. "We make it so the artists can afford to be here. Other places don't do that," Tracy said.

When he and Carol moved there, Jerome wasn't an important place where creative work was happening. If anything, the artists made it such a place. Certainly it had some advantages, but the greatest advantage was that it had been overlooked. It was a cheap place to live, which made it attractive for artists wanting to keep things simple. At the time Tracy moved there, Jerome was also economically stagnant. "The town was basically dead," he recalled, "until the hippies came in and brought this town back to life."

This is not uncommon. Artists often move into rundown parts of towns and transform those areas into popular cultural scenes. As Richard Florida wrote, "The key to economic growth lies not just in the ability to attract the Creative Class, but to translate that underlying advantage into creative economic outcomes." The town itself was not what made Jerome special as much as the artists who came and made their homes there. But even that was not enough. Artists saw possibilities in what was an otherwise stagnant place and turned it into a hot spot. The Creative Class came in and made the town their own, and when they did that, the economy started to bounce back.

The lesson is that when we find ourselves on the outskirts of a community we long to be part of, we have options. Like Tracy Weisel did, we can create the places we need for our work to thrive. So, when we think about where the next "genius cluster" will happen, we may want to look first at the unlikely places in our lives and make the most of the opportunities there.

Embrace Your Place

Not everyone can set sail for another continent or drive across the country on a whim. Most of us have bills to pay and commitments to keep. But does this mean we are unable to do interesting, creative work? Sometimes the scenes we need to be a part of are where we find ourselves right now. Because for every Hemingway in Paris, there's a Brontë in Haworth.

> ## LOOK AT THE UNLIKELY PLACES AND MAKE THE MOST OF THE OPPORTUNITIES THERE.

In the mid-nineteenth century Haworth was a small town in northern England, described by one writer as "a dirty village of weavers' cottages, where death came early." It was a bleak place with few trees and constant wind, and a family named Brontë called it home.

Patrick Brontë was an ambitious young minister from Ireland who had brought his family to Haworth to open a local parish. It was a hard life. There were six children: five girls—Maria, Elizabeth, Charlotte, Emily, and Anne—and a boy named Branwell. Their mother died in 1821 when the children were all under seven years old. In 1824, the girls were sent to school, which was a horrific, abusive experience. The eldest, Maria, was sent home at eleven years old with tuberculosis and died. The same fate visited Elizabeth in June of that year.

Patrick Brontë removed his three remaining daughters from school and brought them back home, where they continued their educations along with their brother who was already home. With their father as teacher, they memorized Bible passages and studied grammar, geography, and history. Reverend Brontë read his children classic works such as Shakespeare's plays and Milton's *Paradise Lost*, and the four pupils soaked in every word. The shelves were filled with Romantic literature and poetry.

One night when returning home from a trip, the reverend brought home a set of toy soldiers for his children. The four siblings invented imaginary kingdoms, using the small figures to act out plays in this made-up world. They drew maps to these fantasy lands and wrote stories, poems, and histories to go along with them. Storytelling was their way of coping with an otherwise harsh world, and it bound them together.

As the Brontë children grew, their lives were even more centered in Haworth. The girls pursued short-lived careers as teachers and governesses but always ended up back home. One day in 1845, Charlotte found a hidden notebook of poems by Emily. She flipped through the book and found verses with a surprising level of skill that "stirred my heart like the sound of a trumpet." Shortly after, Anne came forward with poetry she had written too.

It wasn't long before all three sisters conspired to submit a book of poems for publication under male pseudonyms. The book of poems was published in May 1846 but sold only two copies. Still, they wondered, could they make enough money from writing to live? Since poetry apparently was not the means to literary fame and fortune, the Brontë sisters turned to writing novels.

Two months after publishing their book of poems, the three sisters each submitted a novel. The two from Anne and Emily were accepted, but Charlotte's was turned down seven times. On the seventh attempt, the publisher asked if she had anything else. She did have something: a story about a simple English woman not unlike herself—*Jane Eyre*. The other two books, which Anne and Emily paid to publish, were *Agnes Grey* and *Wuthering Heights*. All three became literary classics.

The Brontës did not have to move to another city to find their success. If anything, they did the exact opposite of Hemingway. But creative breakthroughs don't just happen. You must seek them out, surrounding yourself with the right network to help your work spread. So, what connections did Charlotte, Emily, and Anne have while living in rural England? Certainly not the host of influential artists Hemingway was privy to in Paris. They seemed to possess no scene, no network, no special opportunity. And still, their work endures today.

Where, then, did the Brontës come from?

They came from Haworth, a town so small they were forced

to cling to each other, every day sharing stories with one another. When the eldest surviving Brontë sister, Charlotte, was young, she would write tiny books in a barely legible script that she bound with a small needle and thread, some of which were sixty thousand words long. Like Tracy Weisel and his band of artists, the Brontës had each other, and what opportunity they lacked, they created. It was a self-made genius cluster, and they didn't have to go anywhere to build it.

For years, I longed to be a writer but felt frustrated by my lack of opportunity. Then something changed: I started to embrace my place. Instead of waiting for someone to invite me to something, I began showing up where creative work was already happening. Having moved to Nashville to chase a girl, I noticed how many authors, creatives, and entrepreneurs were emerging from this small but growing city. I started showing up in coffee shops where I knew other writers spent their time. I attended local meet-ups where entrepreneurs and creatives were gathering. The more I engaged with that scene, the more I became part of it, and that soon resulted in friendships that over time grew into a network.

Sometimes the community we need is right in front of us.

A Moveable Feast

Ernest Hemingway once described Paris as "a moveable feast," meaning it could be anywhere, if you knew how to take it with you. Historically, creative work has been contingent on where you lived, but in the New Renaissance, all that is changing.

Sometimes we don't need to leave home. The place where our greatest growth happens is often where we find ourselves right now. But that doesn't mean we succeed by standing still. The genius cluster doesn't just happen—we must create it, cultivate it. Scenes and networks are all around us, but they will not come find us. We must move. Whether that means moving across the room or around the globe, a willingness to step out of our comfort zone is the first step toward finding the place and the people who will help our work thrive.

SOMETIMES THE COMMUNITY WE NEED IS RIGHT IN FRONT OF US.

To begin, put yourself in the places where creativity is already happening. Show up and be seen. Go to a coffee shop or a conference or maybe make the move to a new city altogether. Join the scene, and find that group of people you need to succeed. Just as Hemingway sought out key influencers in Paris, you can seek the influencers and gatekeepers in your own industry. Impress them, become their apprentices, and let them teach you. Win them over, and these people will welcome you into the scene.

These connections do not just happen, though. You must earn the attention of those already established in the scene. How do you do this? Serve them somehow. Use your gifts and talents to help others succeed. This is not sucking up; it's paying your dues and proving your worth. Ernest Hemingway did not just hunt down the most famous authors of his time and pick their brains. He became their friend, offering his services in any way he could—from editing a literary magazine for Ford Maddox Ford to helping Gertrude Stein get published. Vincent van Gogh displayed a similar level of servitude to his peers, as did Tracy Weisel.

Success in any creative field is contingent on the scenes and networks you are a part of. You join the scene, showing up and sharing your work. But you build a network by giving more than you take. A network is not made by just connecting with the right people, but by connecting those people to each other. It's not just who you know—it's who you help. As you make these contributions, what you will create is a group of relationships—a network—that you can take with you wherever you go, just as Hemingway did with Paris.

Chapter 7

COLLABORATE WITH OTHERS

THE STARVING ARTIST WORKS ALONE.
THE THRIVING ARTIST COLLABORATES WITH OTHERS.

Most any significant creative endeavor . . . calls for accomplices.
—PHILIPPE PETIT

WHEN SOMEONE ASKED C. S. LEWIS IF HE HAD INFLUENCED J. R. R. Tolkien, his friend and world-famous author of *The Lord of the Rings* and *The Hobbit*, he laughed. "No one ever influenced Tolkien," he said. "You might as well try to influence a Bandersnatch." A Bandersnatch is a mythical creature that appears in *Through the Looking Glass*. It's an irritable monster, not a creature you'd want to tangle with and certainly not one you could easily "influence."

So, when he said this, people took Lewis at his word. Surely Tolkien was a writer who was stuck in his ways—with his invented languages and made-up mythology—a true lone genius. And for years, that's just what people believed. *No one ever influenced Tolkien.* But that's not the whole story. C. S. Lewis *did* influence Tolkien in some powerful ways, and he wasn't the only one.

"There was a group of them," Diana Glyer said, "nineteen men, and they got together once or twice a week for about seventeen years. And in those meetings, there was a special kind of magic that happened." Glyer teaches English at Azusa Pacific University and has dedicated much of her career to the study of the Inklings, the literary group that included J. R. R. Tolkien, C. S. Lewis, and their friends. One afternoon Professor Glyer told me how they met for decades once a week over tea and pipe smoke. "They read their works in progress to one another," she said, "and they stayed up late into the night giving each other critiques . . . And it is in this forge of friendship and engagement that some of the great works that we love were created. They're not that different, I guess, from a lot of college students talking about what they were working on and then supporting, helping, and encouraging, and challenging each other in the midst of it."

But for a long time, many people had no idea the Inklings were influencing each other's work in such profound ways. When Glyer read that Bandersnatch quote for the first time in high school, it bothered her. "How could these guys interact," she recalled thinking, "talk with each other, go over works in progress, rough drafts of their work together, and to have that happen in conversation for there not to be influence?" And so began a decades-long dive into the world of the Inklings, exploring how this community of writers influenced some of the greatest works of literature of the twentieth century.

Among the many examples Professor Glyer cited of how these men influenced each other's work, one in particular stood out. After the unexpected success of *The Hobbit*, J. R. R. Tolkien's publisher asked him to write another novel. As he began writing what was then called *The New Hobbit*, he got stuck only a few chapters in. One day he asked his friend C. S. Lewis to lunch and admitted to feeling bored with the project. "I don't know what to do," Tolkien said. "I think I'm done."

"The problem," Lewis replied, "is that hobbits are only interesting when they're in un-hobbit-like situations." That was all he needed to say.

"So," Glyer explained, "because of one lunch with a buddy, the story where Tolkien was basically done and directionless, one comment opens up the vista and gives us what we now know as this wonderful, rich epic story, *The Lord of the Rings*. I think that's pretty strong evidence of influence."

With one little comment, C. S. Lewis changed the direction of what would become his friend's greatest work. As Lewis himself once wrote, "The next best thing to being wise oneself is to live in a circle of those who are." The same, it seems, can be said for being creative. We don't do our best work alone; we do it by collaborating with others.

THE RULE OF COLLABORATION

Beyoncé's sixth studio album, *Lemonade*, was released on April 23, 2016, and credited seventy-two writers. When people learned about this, there was significant public backlash. One person on Twitter wrote, "Is this the time of year where we call Beyoncé a musical genius even though she has 50–100 writers and producers for each album?" Another said, "Beyoncé has FIFTEEN writers on one of her songs. But she's a genius, they say."

> WE DON'T DO OUR BEST WORK ALONE.

This raises an important question: Do geniuses work alone? The implication in these comments is yes. We often believe groundbreaking creative work happens in isolation—a remote cabin in the woods, a secluded laboratory out in the middle of nowhere, a music studio in some dilapidated building in the inner city. But is this the way creativity really works?

We hold in our minds a certain picture of a professional artist as a lone creator, some solitary genius who executes a vision all by himself, slaving away at the work with only his thoughts and brilliance to keep him company. But this is a gross misunderstanding of how real artists get their work done. As creativity researcher Keith Sawyer says, "You cannot be creative alone. Isolated individuals are not creative. That's not how creativity happens."

When fans discovered how many collaborators Beyoncé had, the overall sentiment was that she was getting more credit than she deserved. Why? Because she didn't write those songs all by herself. This is not an uncommon reaction. When we realize our favorite author or filmmaker didn't create their masterwork alone, we are disappointed, maybe even disillusioned. There's something about the story of the solitary genius we want to cling to, however misguided it may be. "That's a really nice story," Diana Glyer said. But such a picture of genius "robs writers and other creatives of the possibility of writing the way that writing or creating normally takes place, which is in community."

Kanye West's *The Life of Pablo* credits more than a hundred writers. Rihanna's *Anti* credits more than thirty. Are these individuals not real artists? If we allow ourselves to accept the new definition of *artist* not as a lone genius but as a visionary who brings people and resources together, this creates opportunities for our work to flourish. The New Renaissance is not about working in isolation; it's about finding more ways to collaborate with other like-minded creatives. Our success is closely related to our ability to work well with others.

This is the Rule of Collaboration, which says genius happens in groups. Starving Artists work alone, but Thriving Artists collaborate with others.

GENIUS HAPPENS IN GROUPS

Creative output is a slog that is often slower and more grueling than we would like and at times can feel discouraging. The best artists, or the smart ones at least, tend to involve other people "because," as Diana Glyer told me, "the life of an artist, any kind of creator, is fraught with discouragement. You need people to correct your path."

Your greatest work will not come from just you. In my interviews with hundreds of working creatives, I discovered that many professional artists do not work alone. Yes, they may retreat to a solitary location to finish a book or record an album, but their work is always refined by community. Many of the most significant creative breakthroughs in history were not inventions by individuals. They were the result of a small group of people working together. These creations came about thanks to what Michael Farrell calls "collaborative circles." In his research, Farrell credits such groups for everything from the invention of psychotherapy to the birth of French Impressionism. Genius, he argues, tends to happen in community, not isolation. This was true of J. R. R. Tolkien, C. S. Lewis, and their group of writers—and it's true for us today.

As we begin to grasp the importance of relationships in creative work, we must address the question: What do we do with these connections? We use them. Not in an exploitive way, but in a collaborative way. "A certain kind of magic" is how Diana Glyer described the events at those late-night meetings at Oxford University where the Inklings met. These writers were influential because they under-stood the power of collaboration. Creativity is not a solitary invention but a collaborative creation. Community offers opportunities for creative work to thrive, and that is a kind of magic we can all create.

FIND YOUR FELLOW MISFITS

When Alfred Hair, a young black man living in south Florida, graduated high school in 1961, his dream was to become a million-aire by his thirty-first birthday. But how could he do such a thing, living in the segregated south at a time when African Americans had little chance of upward social mobility? At the same time, a white painter named A. E. Backus had been teaching art classes to a group of children that had included Hair ever since he was in ninth grade.

> # CREATIVITY IS NOT A SOLITARY INVENTION BUT A COLLABORATIVE CREATION.

Backus taught Hair the essentials to painting, but when the fledgling artist saw how much money his teacher was making, he saw an opportunity. Since Backus was charging $250 per paint-ing, Hair thought he could paint ten paintings in the same amount of time it took his teacher to paint one. Then, he could charge an affordable rate of twenty-five dollars and if he pulled this off, he could make the same hourly rate as his mentor. It almost seemed too good to be true.

While this was happening, another black man named Harold Newton was elsewhere selling Florida landscape paintings door to door. Indirectly influenced by Backus, Newton had become a master at direct sales. When Hair saw Newton's door-to-door selling and the money Backus was bringing in, he combined the two strategies to start selling paintings door to door. He would collect the money even before the oil on the canvas had dried.

By his early twenties, Alfred Hair was already driving a Cadillac.

The people of Fort Pierce, Florida, began to notice how a young man in their community was making a name for himself with art, and soon others wanted in on the action. An attractive, charismatic young man, Hair enlisted twenty-six other painters in his money-making venture—all African Americans, none with any formal art training, and many just as eager to succeed. This group of painters came to be known as the Florida Highwaymen.

The Florida Highwaymen shared a common aesthetic, with each painter bringing something unique to the group. They were young and energetic and all very poor. Other than what Hair had picked up from Backus, they had no teachers except each other, or as the only female in the group, Mary Ann Carroll, said, they learned "from one another's brushes."

At night, they would get together and paint as many pieces as they could, then go out the next day and try to sell them. "They'd go to real estate brokerages, stock market brokerages, courthouses, and banks," Gary Monroe, the biographer of the Florida Highwaymen, told me, "and they would sell fifteen to twenty paintings. They'd come back [at the end of the day] with zero paintings and a pocketful of money." Who bought the artwork? Nearly everyone. The canvases appealed to the postwar audience that was flocking to Florida in the 1950s, dreaming of paradise. Through evocative scenes and bright, colorful sunsets, the Highwaymen's paintings spoke to the ideal of a better life and offered a sense of security, as if to say, "everything is going to be all right." And the paintings, according to Monroe, "sold like hotcakes."

For some of them, it was money driven. Art was a means to crawl out of the seemingly inescapable poverty they faced every day. It was a chance to break out of that life and create a new one for themselves. Alfred Hair "could paint as good as he wanted and as fast as he wanted," Monroe explained, "but he wanted to paint fast because that made the money roll in more quickly." Other members of the group aspired to do more meaningful work with their painting, but regardless of the reason, all they had was each other. And they relied heavily on that community to help their art succeed.

The Highwaymen practiced together. They worked together. They went out on the streets and sold together. They even competed to see who could sell the most paintings each day. But no matter what, each member worked hard to support the group. These artists learned from and influenced one another in such profound ways that it's unlikely any single one of them would have succeeded alone.

This was the early 1960s in the Deep South, and a band of black painters were challenging social conventions the civil rights movement hadn't even touched yet. They did not have any natural advantage. But this drove them to one another, and that collaboration made all the difference. In the words of Gary Monroe, Alfred Hair was "living the dream that Martin Luther King was just about to commit to paper for his iconic 'I Have a Dream' speech." These artists couldn't afford to work in isolation—they needed one another too much. Rejection brought them together. Even when they were competing, they were collaborating, spurring one another on toward success.

The Florida Highwaymen produced an estimated two hundred thousand paintings during the course of a few decades. Though these works initially sold for tens of dollars, today they are worth thousands of dollars and hang on the walls of the homes of people like Steven Spielberg. Alfred Hair and his cohorts created something, albeit by accident, that was so powerful and interesting that historians have called it the "last great art movement of the twentieth century."

The Florida Highwaymen were misfits. It was not easy for these artists to succeed at a time when black men and women were afforded few opportunities to advance in society. But they didn't let such inequities disqualify them from success. If anything, that fueled them. They used the fact that they were outcasts; it made them rely on one another. And because of that collaboration, they were able to accomplish something greater than each person could have done alone.

Community made possible what was otherwise impossible for the individual.

LET COMPETITION DRIVE YOU

Most of us prefer the image of the solitary genius alone in his studio, painting a masterpiece. This is what we have been conditioned to picture when we hear the term *artist*. An artist works alone. Right? But this picture of a man against the world is most often a myth; in fact, it wasn't even true of Michelangelo, the stereotypical "lone genius." What drove him was not just collaboration but competition.

Renaissance Italy was not the quaint community of artists we see in Romantic times and thereafter. Nor was it the collaborative community of the Impressionists in Paris or the Inklings at Oxford. It was the age of the courtier, when artists and politicians alike had to learn how to maneuver and manipulate their way into power. An awareness of who was around you and how to use those resources to succeed was essential.

A sense of competition often drives our collaboration, even when we don't realize that's what is happening. To be creative, you must break away from what is expected, essentially competing with what has come before so that you can create something new. But you can't do this alone. It's too discouraging. So, you connect with peers who share your ideals and who resonate with your work. After that it is only a matter of time before you begin comparing your work to theirs. This is not a bad thing, however. This is how you get better. All art requires some level of healthy competition to make the creator a true master. And this requires some gumption, an attitude that goes beyond meekness but doesn't quite become arrogance.

Michelangelo was the perfect candidate for success in such a competitive climate. He was notorious for sizing himself up against others, constantly trying to prove himself. This began, most notably, with a public competition in 1504 between Michelangelo and Leonardo da Vinci, an artist at the time who was more established and twice Michelangelo's age. Despite giving his best effort, Michelangelo lost the contest but never forgot the experience. For the rest of his life, he would strive to be better than his predecessors, to surpass the work of the greats who came before him.

At times we all feel a little competitive. We may even experience a slight twinge of jealousy of a friend's success or feel threatened by it. It does no good to wish such feelings away. Instead, use that energy. Let it drive you to create and do better work. You don't need to fear the accomplishments of others, but don't ignore other people's success either. Pay attention to what your peers are doing, and then let that awareness sharpen your focus so that you can improve.

Great work does not happen in a vacuum. We must have an aware-ness of what others are doing and a certain level of competition to keep us sharp and continually growing as artists.

What Michelangelo learned first as a competitor—that when you put creative people together or even pit them against one another, the result is better work—he eventually put to work when he undertook a massive project later in life.

In the summer of 1525, when the artist was fifty years old, he was working on the Medici Chapel and Laurentian Library. More than a hundred stoneworkers worked for him as he served as chief architect of the Basilica di San Lorenzo. He managed a messy work site, a large labor force, and a complex business operation. For the last forty years of his life, Michelangelo oversaw hundreds of employees who helped him. He kept track of every detail, every scrap of paper, and recorded it all—even the purchasing of raw materials.

He was an artist in the same way Steve Jobs or Jim Henson were artists. They didn't physically make each of the products for which they were ultimately given credit, but they are no less responsible for those creations. These skills of leading, managing, and collabo-rating with peers can be just as important in a creative career as the inspiration side of things, and no less creative.

Hire Help

Sometimes we need more than just a loose collective of peers to help us succeed. We need a more formal group of coworkers, a team to help us realize our vision. And that, too, is the job of an artist.

After fifteen years of working in a career in manufactur-ing, design, and construction, Caroline Robinson quit her job and launched a business. She had been a creative her whole life, but now it was time to go out on her own, and she intuitively knew she needed more than just herself to make that happen. Having carefully planned a career that would allow her to "be arty and still make money," she decided to become a cartographer. "I leapt in with two feet!" she shouted in a delightful English accent from her home in Cornwall, United Kingdom. But then reality set in, and "three months in, I went, 'Oh, my God, what have I done? Oh, no!'"

Clear Mapping Company, a cartographic design consultancy, grew rapidly, and it wasn't long before success overwhelmed Caroline, threatening to swallow her creativity whole. Then she had to make an important decision: Would she be "just an artist" or would she learn how to manage a team so she could get the help she needed?

What Caroline did next is important, because this intersection is one we may encounter in our own careers, and what we do will very likely affect our work for years, maybe even decades. She didn't push through the challenge on her own; instead, she reached out to friends and family, leveraging her personal network and hired help. When we imagine a full-time artist like Caroline, we probably picture someone laboring over a drawing-board, alone, working into the wee hours of the night. We picture the final product, the book, the map, the painting. Whatever we picture, it probably looks nothing like the way Caroline Robinson actually spends her time, working collaboratively with her clients and employees.

Today Caroline manages a team of three people and is currently looking for a senior illustrator to add to her payroll. Her job, as she sees it, is to always be looking for new talent and future opportunities to grow the business. The work she and her team does is "not about credit," she told me; it's about the collaboration.

"I may start with a gem of an idea," she said, "but by letting go and letting other people bring that idea to life, we end up with a better product. I don't worry about who is influencing the creative aspect because it's all about making it work for the client. When we work together, the end product is stronger anyway."

MAKING A MASTERMIND

Creativity needs collaboration. From the critical jabs of the Inklings to the friendly competition of the Florida Highwaymen to the more intentional leadership Michelangelo demonstrated with his forty-year assignment at San Lorenzo, what we learn from each of these artists is that without others' help, we do not produce our best work.

The product may be a book or a church or even a map. Whatever it is, we won't do our best work without a community that under-stands our work and can hold us accountable. We need people who resonate with our art and have the courage to tell us when we can do better.

Four years ago, three people I barely knew got together and decided they wanted to start a peer group of local business leaders. Each person asked three other people to join the group, and that's how twelve of us started meeting together every week to discuss our businesses and lives. We've been doing it ever since.

This group is not a collective of famous people or successful entrepreneurs. Most of the members were just at the beginning stages of their careers when it began. In fact, you could even say we were a bunch of misfits, not really fitting in anywhere else. So, we formed a circle of a dozen peers and started meeting to share our hopes and dreams with each other. I can say without a doubt, this group has been the single greatest source of professional and personal growth for me in the past decade.

Something similar happened when I finally hired a handful of employees to help me run my business as a writer and online writing teacher. At first it was hard, because I was accustomed to working alone. This is what we are told artists do, after all. But the more I embraced my need for community, the more I saw how powerful working with others can be.

CREATIVITY NEEDS COLLABORATION

If you want to do world-changing creative work, you must reconcile the fact that you likely won't be able to do it alone. You need help. Find your band of misfits, use the accountability of that group, and let your sense of competition drive you to create better work.

Diana Glyer's personal theory is that 92 percent of *The Lord of the Rings* was written on Wednesday nights, because J. R. R. Tolkien knew on Thursdays he'd have to face his friend C. S. Lewis and account for his work. Lewis and the rest of the Inklings would ask where Tolkien was in the story he'd been telling them. "What did you write?" they would ask.

"And it's that expectation," Professor Glyer said, "there's a ferocious aspect to it. But there's also compassionate expectation that says, 'You have this great idea. You told me about this project. You said you were going to drive this. How's that going for you?' And knowing that other people are out there, I think, makes all the difference."

Chapter 8

PRACTICE IN PUBLIC

⇉ THE STARVING ARTIST DOESN'T SHARE HIS WORK.
THE THRIVING ARTIST PRACTICES IN PUBLIC. ⇇

Play always as if in the presence of a master.
—ROBERT SCHUMANN

EVEN BEFORE SHE LEARNED HER LETTERS, STEPHANIE HALLIGAN was drawing pictures. As a child, her dream was to be a Looney Tunes or Disney animator. "If you were to ask my friends and family," she said, "I was meant to be a cartoonist." As an adult, however, she lost that drive to create. Starting in high school and continuing through college, Stephanie's concerns shifted to more practical matters. How would she make a living? What would she do to pay bills? What kind of job would she have? Drawing cartoons was no longer at the top of the priority list.

Leaving college with $34,579 in debt, the young graduate got a job at a financial-literacy nonprofit, helping students and low-income families how to save money. It was rewarding work, but like many others, she started her career with a sense of purpose that only carried her so far. Three years into that job, Stephanie's passion had waned, and she felt like something was missing—something important.

The job was gratifying, but still Stephanie wanted *more*. Exactly what she was missing, she couldn't say, but that *something* refused to leave her alone. "It felt like that creative piece of me didn't have a place to go," she recalled. So she poured her energy into a blog and launched the *Empowered Dollar* in May 2012, detailing her experience of getting out of debt. She worked on that project for two years before adding an important piece to it: cartoons.

Using her talent for drawing, Stephanie began illustrating the topics she was writing about. It was an experiment, which made the success of the effort that much more surprising. But when her mother heard Stephanie was doing this, she said, "Of course!" It just made sense. She'd seen Stephanie make art ever since she was a little girl, so it didn't come as a shock. Sometimes our most obvious gifts are the hardest for us to recognize.

> ## SOMETIMES OUR MOST OBVIOUS GIFTS ARE THE HARDEST FOR US TO RECOGNIZE.

It was a powerful time for Stephanie. "Something in me came back to life," she recalled. Adding cartoons to the blog grew the young artist's confidence and taught her that she had something valuable to offer, something beyond the demands of a day job. But up until this point, drawing was still a hobby. In 2014, Stephanie's friend Noah asked what an ideal day would look like for her, and when her answer had more to do with cartooning than personal finance, she knew something had to change.

Noah challenged her. If this was what she wanted to do for a living, why wasn't she doing it? Could she sell a cartoon in the next seventy-two hours? It was an odd dare, but the audacity of it excited her. Seventy-two hours to sell a cartoon? She was game for anything.

Stephanie sent off a quick note to her list of e-mail newsletter subscribers with a simple message: she had three cartoon prints for sale. "Do you want one?" was the e-mail subject line. The pieces were forty-five dollars each, and within twenty-four hours Stephanie had sold her first one.

"It was," she said, "the first time ever that I put that equation together, that my cartoons could equal money. From that moment on, I knew my only job was . . . to create work I cared about and then put it out into the world for sale."

On January 1, 2015, Stephanie started a second blog called *Art to Self*, which was a personal project, a public commitment to draw every day. It was also a testament to what got her to the point of being a full-time artist in the first place: sharing her work. Today, Stephanie does illustrations for universities, nonprofits, and major banks. She's done whiteboard animations for start-ups and small-business owners and continues to inspire a growing audience through what she calls "motivational cartoons," which she publishes on her blog.

One of her cartoons features a white ghost with the caption: "Let yourself be seen." Below it, Stephanie wrote, "I was nervous about putting my work out in the open. Because as much as I wanted people to know what I was doing, I was worried about being exposed. There was a risk of letting myself be seen. Like if they looked too closely, they'd discover I was a fraud. If I showed off my work, I'd be vulnerable to criticism or worse: silence. But if I embraced the risk that came with being seen, there was a huge reward waiting for me: the feeling of acknowledgment, of being noticed, of feeling heard. And most important, feeling worthy of being seen. That seemed so worth the risk."

If Stephanie had never put her drawings out there for people to see, she never would have made money from her art. She'd still be dreaming of being a cartoonist someday. And this is something we can all learn from. Promotion isn't something an artist avoids; it's an essential part of the job.

SHARE YOUR WORK

The novelist George Sand once wrote that it is the duty of all artists "to find an adequate expression to convey [their art] to as many souls as possible." Or to put it more succinctly: art needs an audience.

Often I hear writers and creatives complaining about having to market themselves. They are, it seems, afraid of appearing sleazy or "self-promotional," which is understandable. We are attracted to art because it feels pure, so we worry that if we fixate too much on fame or success that such ambition may ruin the purity of our work. We want to believe that if we do our jobs well enough that the audience will just find us. But that's not how it works.

> # PROMOTION ISN'T SOMETHING AN ARTIST AVOIDS; IT'S AN ESSENTIAL PART OF THE JOB.

If you build it, they will not come. Austin Kleon writes, "In order to be found, you have to be findable." You must put your work in front of the people who will react to it.

But how?

We all need our work to resonate with someone; our art needs an audience. The way the Starving Artist attempts this is by working in private, secretly hoping to be discovered some day. She spurns the need for an audience and chooses to suffer for her work instead, holding out for that lucky moment when someone stumbles upon her genius. The Thriving Artist, on the other hand, chooses a different path: she shares her work by practicing in public. Not by being sleazy or self-promotional but by letting people simply watch her work.

Stephanie Halligan transitioned from dreaming of drawing cartoons to becoming a full-time artist through a gradual process, but it began with sharing her work. This act of generosity helped her build an audience around her artwork, which made everything else possible. At the outset, however, her readers were not many, but that was just fine with her because she was using the experience to grow. "On one hand," she said of her blog, "it's a self-serving project that holds me accountable to doing art. And at the same time, it's been amazing to see how people have connected with my cartoons. It's also a place for me to share about the moments I'm experiencing. It's the messages I need to hear."

As she shared more of her work, Stephanie's client base grew. One daily drawing was a two-panel comic depicting the dream of being an entrepreneur with a picture of herself riding a unicorn, crooning, "Freedom forever!" versus the reality of running a business, which included a picture of her hunched over a laptop, scowling and saying, "I haven't showered." It was this kind of honesty that endeared Stephanie to an audience.

This is what happens when we practice in public: we not only hone our abilities but attract an audience interested in what we're sharing.

The more we do this, the better we get, and the more confident we become. Eventually, people start to notice. This doesn't mean we let them see every step of the process, but we have to put our work out there. And when we do, we just might be surprised at how people react.

When we show the world our ideas as they unfold to us, people repay such generosity. Because she shared her work, Stephanie's audience responded with the same openness and vulnerability she shared. First they gave their attention; then they gave their money. All because she wasn't doing her work in private, hoping to get discovered. Instead, she was doing what all Thriving Artists do: she was practicing in public.

THE RULE OF THE AUDIENCE

In the early 1900s, creative minds from all over Europe flocked to a windmill-covered community located on the outskirts of Paris. The place was called Montmartre, which means "Mount of Martyrs," named after the hill on which it was located. And it was here that the modern art movement was born.

This northern Parisian neighborhood became a haven for Starving Artists. Fleeing the traditional values of their parents, they sought a new way of life, spurning the pursuit of money, fame, and luxury. This was a new era, and these creatives proudly suffered for their art. "Art for art's sake" was the motto of these Bohemians who willingly embraced poverty and obscurity.

Montmartre was a community of artists who sacrificed themselves for their work, giving up worldly comforts so they could create something pure. Some even wore this suffering as a badge of honor, believing it somehow made their work better. Among these artists was a young man from Spain who began his career drawing prostitutes and clowns he met in the cabarets and cafés. He once said his goal was to "live like a pauper, but with plenty of money." The artist's name was Pablo Ruiz Picasso.

Picasso was not alone in his aspiration to have it both ways: to be a serious artist but also have the means to live however he wanted. To starve may represent a certain commitment to one's art, but no one wants to suffer. At the same time, no one wants to toot his own horn. Many of us would prefer to do our work quietly without any hype or hoopla and just let the fans come to us. But that's a myth.

This brings us to the Rule of the Audience, which says that before art can have an impact, it must first have an audience. No one is exempt from this rule, not even Picasso.

As a recent art school graduate, Picasso began his career in 1899 by meeting other artists in Barcelona at the local cafés and bars. Els Quatre Gats, a large tavern decorated with traditional Spanish tiles, was the place he frequented most often. Located in a narrow cobbled alley, tucked in between the high buildings in a less-fashionable part of town, it was the perfect place for artists to gather and share their work. Picasso began visiting the tavern at age seventeen. He hosted his first exhibition there and made a poster that served as the restaurant's menu cover. Even as a teenager, he was putting his work on display for all to see.

In 1900, Picasso decided to relocate to Paris, understanding the need to put his work in the places where opportunity was greatest. In 1905 he met the writer Gertrude Stein and offered to paint her. Soon the two were meeting daily, and Stein would later claim to have sat for ninety sessions with Picasso. An avid art collector, Stein championed his work for decades, helping Picasso get it in front of the right people.

Thriving Artists do more than bloom where they're planted; they put their work where it has the greatest potential to succeed. In Picasso's case, that meant sharing his work. "Picasso was very good about giving his work to the right collectors," wrote Sue Hostetler, editor in chief of *Art Basel Miami Beach* magazine. "He was smart enough to see that during his time the savviest collectors were in Paris and he knew that if these collectors had his art it would support the value."

When Picasso offered to paint Gertrude Stein, he must have known how influential she was in the Parisian art scene. And, the dedication he had to filling her home with his art, something she would boast about for years, was the perfect example of making his work findable.

What launched Picasso's career, transitioning him from obscure artist to one of the most famous painters of the twentieth century, was a willingness to put himself out there. He did not always reveal each step of his creative process, but practicing in public became a lifelong habit for the artist. While others were living in obscurity in Montmartre, he was planting his work where it had the greatest opportunity to flourish, and that's something we all can do.

PERFORMANCE IS STILL PRACTICE

The comedian Chris Rock has a habit of showing up unannounced in small nightclubs. No one in the audience knows he's coming. They haven't bought a ticket to see him; they aren't even aware he will be performing. Then he takes the stage, and in front of an audience of fifty or so people, he goes through his forty-five-minute routine.

With legal notepad in hand, Rock offers the material in an informal and unexaggerated voice, seeing which jokes connect and which ones fall flat. This is far from the polished, outlandish version of Chris Rock we are used to seeing on TV comedy specials. Most of the jokes fail, and the audience is left feeling underwhelmed. And that's by design.

When he's working on new material, Rock may do this forty to fifty times in preparation for a big tour. At a small New Jersey club near his home, he'll randomly walk in, take the stage, and bomb. He's not doing his usual bits but instead trying out new ones. Sometimes it goes so poorly that people get up and leave. Other times they fold their arms or laugh *at* him, not *with* him. Why does he subject himself to such humiliation? Because Chris Rock didn't become Chris Rock by practicing his jokes in a dressing room. He did it by taking the stage and failing in front of a live audience. The same goes for Louis CK and Steve Martin. This was even how musician Beck Hansen began his career: performing for audiences who didn't want to hear a white kid singing folk songs in a rock and roll club.

There is no better way to improve than to put your work out there—sharing it for the whole world to see—no other way to get discovered than to risk rejection. You have to practice in public.

I used to want to be a professional musician. After practicing the guitar in my parents' basement for six years, I wasn't much better than when I started. I made incremental improvements but was nowhere near proficient. But then I joined a band, and we began playing shows, one after another, each time getting a little better. By the time I graduated college, I was on my fourth band and first major tour.

THERE IS NO BETTER WAY TO IMPROVE THAN TO PUT YOUR WORK OUT THERE, NO OTHER WAY TO GET DISCOVERED THAN TO RISK REJECTION.

For a year I traveled through North America in a van with six other musicians, playing sometimes several shows a day. During that time I became better than I ever thought possible. Turns out, this is the best kind of practice: sharing your work with others. It's how we all earn attention for our work and grow as artists.

You don't do your best work at rehearsal. You do your best when you have to: when you're on stage in front of a live audience, when the publisher is waiting for the manuscript, when everyone is waiting for you to step up. Everything else is prologue. That's not to say we shouldn't pursue excellence or that we prematurely step into the spotlight. But it does mean the way we hone our craft is by doing it—not talking about it or studying it, but by getting to work. Thriving Artists do not wait for these opportunities to share; they seek them out.

Of course this means we will eventually encounter failure. But in every failure and disappointment, there is an opportunity to either give in to frustration or see such shortcomings as practice. In the words of Chris Rock, these failures teach us; they are our "training camps." You can't avoid these moments; they are necessary steps on the road to greatness. When we fail, we can see our failures as early end points or as training for what's to come.

This is deeper than silver-lining thinking. It's a commitment to persevere, believing one setback will not defeat you. You'll live to fight another day, and you will be better because of it. And today? Well, that was just practice for the next time. The next show, the next book, the next chance to do it better, when the stakes are even higher. The sooner you get started, the more prepared you'll be. To do the work of a professional, you have to stop waiting to be seen and start sharing your work now.

PARTNER WITH THE AUDIENCE

Sometimes, though, the way we get attention is not by tooting our own horns but by concealing our efforts to be seen. Let's take one of the most successful rock albums of all time as an example: *Led Zeppelin IV.*

The year was 1971, and Led Zeppelin was at the height of its career. The British super group had formed only a few years before and was already one of the most popular touring acts in the world, recently dethroning the Beatles as Best Group in the prestigious annual Readers Poll of *Melody Maker.*

> TO DO THE WORK OF A PROFESSIONAL, YOU HAVE TO STOP WAITING TO BE SEEN AND START SHARING YOUR WORK NOW.

The band, however, was heavily criticized and considered by some critics to not be a real rock and roll band. *Rolling Stone* said their work "doesn't challenge anybody's intelligence or sensibilities" and called the band "as ephemeral as Marvel comix." Others said they were mostly hype and not nearly as talented as everyone thought, what with their lavishly long concerts and dazzling displays of showmanship. This gave Jimmy Page, the mastermind behind the band, an idea.

At the pinnacle of their success, when they were about to un-officially claim the title of best rock band in the world, Led Zeppelin took a risk and released their fourth record anonymously. Neither the band's name nor any of the musicians' names would appear any-where on the album.

Imagine the insanity of doing something like this now, much less in the 1970s without the existence of the Internet and other media outlets. This was unheard of. In an era of one-hit wonders when rock bands came and went practically overnight, the risk was considerable. Such a willingness to put their work out in the world without a name or brand anywhere on it was brave, if not a little reckless.

Atlantic Records protested the idea, but the group was adamant. They were being accused of building a career off of hype, so the decision was obvious: they had to remove the name. "We wanted to demonstrate that it was the music that made Zeppelin popular," Jimmy Page later said. "It had nothing to do with our name or image." The packaging included a picture of a man with a bundle of sticks on his back and some strange symbols where the band credits normally would appear.

This was more than just a humility play, though. It was a genius marketing move. Months beforehand and after the stunt was pulled, Zeppelin took out ads teasing the fact that they had a new, unnamed record. At shows, they told fans of their new release but refused to give details. This refusal must have created an insatiable curiosity that drove the staunchest of fans to find it. How long do you think it took fans to make the discovery? My guess is not long. Imagine being one of the first people to locate the record in a store and buy it, only to discover it was one of the world's most famous rock groups. What would you do next? Probably tell everyone you knew.

This is the record that brought the world "Stairway to Heaven" and other timeless hits. Without a doubt, it is one of the greatest rock albums of all time, and here it was, on the shelf at a record store, nameless. Locating it, for some teenage music junkie, would have felt like discovering the Holy Grail. Apparently, that's what happened, because the record sold more than twenty-three million copies, and today remains one of the top three bestselling albums in history.

Who do you think first found that record? It was not some random listener who happened to discover *Led Zeppelin IV* in the record stores. The established fans of Led Zeppelin went in search of it. Had the band not spent years sharing their work, the record almost certainly would have flopped. Yet the band's ability to build such an avid fan base and then use those fans to drive their biggest release led to their success. Even the best art needs an audience. Not to mention, they had been practicing in public for years at this point. Jimmy Page had been playing as a talented studio musician since his early teens, and the rest of the group were all established in their own respective disciplines.

When you practice like that, sharing your work for the world to see, you develop more than just a reputation. You build a legitimate fan base around your work. And when you've done that, you've created a powerful asset. Led Zeppelin offered their music to the world as a gift and partnered with their audience to share it. For years, they'd been experimenting with new forms of rock—all in front of an audience. And here was the greatest experiment yet. Could their art live without their name attached to it? Apparently, it could, but perhaps the bigger question is, could it have succeeded without the audience? I doubt it.

The Point Is the Practice

When Stephanie Halligan finally mustered the courage to ask her fans to buy her work, she was surprised they said yes. But that's because the hardest work was done. For years, she had been illustrating her blog with cartoons, and just as with Led Zeppelin, all that practice adds up to something—not just the attention of an audience but the skill to support it. Even the most generous of audiences will not tolerate an amateur.

Stephanie drew a daily cartoon for two years. She did it every day, without fail, understanding that the practice enables her to be where she is today. And because of that practice, she was able to realize her childhood dream of becoming a cartoonist. It's not just the fact she did her work in public that made it happen. It's that she practiced, gradually getting better and allowing her audience to see that progress.

EVEN THE MOST GENEROUS OF AUDIENCES WILL NOT TOLERATE AN AMATEUR.

When we sincerely offer our gifts to the world, not through hype but by practicing in public, the world often repays us by first taking notice and then responding with loyalty. We get better, earning an audience that will allow us to continue creating for years to come.

Part 3

MONEY

IF WE ARE GOING TO THRIVE AS ARTISTS, WE CANNOT MERELY SURvive. We have to make a living off our creations, which means at some point we need to talk about the part we're all uncomfortable discussing: money. The Starving Artist avoids this at all costs, but the Thriving Artist understands that business is part of art and even money is something an artist must master.

Chapter 9

Don't Work for Free

> The Starving Artist works for free.
> The Thriving Artist always works for something.

When bankers get together for dinner, they discuss Art. When artists get together for dinner, they discuss Money.
—Oscar Wilde

IN SCHOOL, MELISSA DINWIDDIE HAD ALWAYS MADE GOOD GRADES in English. But when she found herself trapped in the paralysis of perfectionism that prevented her from writing anything, she knew that wasn't going to work. To procrastinate, she started making visual art, with making money as the furthest thing from her mind.

Within a few months, however, Melissa started fantasizing about turning her art into a business. "I didn't think of myself as an artist at that time," she admitted, "but making things with my hands and playing around with arts and crafts led to its own career path." Her best friend Amy asked her to do a piece that she could give as a gift. Melissa didn't want to charge anything because she needed to fill her portfolio and knew her friend couldn't afford the price she'd want to charge. But Amy insisted, so the two settled on a price of twenty-five dollars. Amy said that's what she would have spent on a similar piece at Target. Melissa spent forty hours on that one piece, and to this day, she still has the crisp one-dollar bill her friend sent her, with "Melissa's first artistic sale" written on it.

Not long after this, Melissa fell in love with the art of calligraphy. She dreamed of creating ketubah art for Jewish wedding ceremonies. A ketubah is a prenuptial document that lists the rights and responsibilities of both the groom and bride, and the document itself is a work of art.

Before the digital revolution and long before high-quality printing became accessible to anyone, a ketubah was often made by hand, always incorporating beautiful calligraphy and hand-lettering. Because this art was such a niche market, it seemed like a viable way for Melissa to earn an income.

Sure enough, just a couple of years after starting with calligraphy, she was commissioned to create her first ketubah for seven hundred dollars. It was, however, dozens of hours of work, which translated to not much of a living wage. Still, making money making art was a revolutionary concept for her.

At the time, Melissa's husband was supporting both of them financially, so she didn't worry about making a living. Her art was more of a hobby, with just enough income to pay for her supplies, weekend workshops, and annual conferences. But when she and her husband divorced, Melissa realized she needed to find a way to make a living with her art.

"I needed an identity," she told me about the difficult time after her divorce. It wasn't enough for her just to make things—she had to make things of value, things people wanted. So the custom ketubah art transitioned to selling ketubah prints, which eventually led to the business she has now, which is helping other people find and reclaim their own creative passions.

"My mission on the planet," she told me, "is to get people creating." Personally, she doesn't care if people want to make money from their creative efforts, "but a lot of people do want to generate income from their creative thing."

Today Melissa Dinwiddie still calls herself an artist, but she's also now an author and speaker. In addition to selling her art online, she runs an online community for women creatives, leads creativity retreats, and brings her experience as a performing artist to workshops, keynotes, and seminars for organizations and corporations. And now that she's doing this full-time she can't imagine going back to working for free. Once she crossed that threshold and began charging what she was worth, her confidence grew.

"Other people may not like your art," she said, "or they may sneer at it for being 'commercial art,' rather than 'fine art,' but for me, making a living from my art was indisputable proof that I was an artist. I am making a living therefore nobody can dispute that I'm an artist."

Melissa's story is confirmation that at some point you have to let people pay you, and for many of us, this is a discipline. Of course, we don't have to make a living from our art to be an artist, but there is, in Melissa's words, "something affirming about getting paid to do what you love." Creative success is about getting to do your work without constraint. Money is not the point, but it is part of the road we all must walk to become professionals. Charging brings dignity to our work. It validates our offering to the world. And it allows us to keep working.

THE RULE OF VALUE

At some point, when you do an activity you love, you might ask, "Could I do this for a *living*?" The next question is, what would you have to compromise? Maybe nothing. You *can* make money making art, and you don't have to sell out to do it. This won't just happen, though. In Melissa's words, you have to "make friends with the business and marketing side of things." You have to be willing to do the job of an artist, which includes more than just making things—it means charging what you're worth.

➤ CHARGING BRINGS DIGNITY TO OUR WORK. ◀

Few of us, especially when we're starting out, are comfortable asking for money to do something we enjoy. Creatives, in particular, get in the habit of doing free gigs in hopes of building a portfolio, and the world does little to dissuade us from such madness. We are told to offer our services at no charge in exchange for "exposure" or because "it's a good opportunity." But is this really the way to start a career?

Recently a study into the popularity of unpaid internships explored this question. For three years, the National Association of Colleges and Employers had been asking graduating seniors whether they received a job offer after a paid or unpaid internship, and for three years the results were the same. Unpaid internships don't give college grads an advantage at all. In fact, more often than not, these unpaid "opportunities" put them at a disadvantage.

Out of the ninety-two hundred students surveyed, 63.1 percent of those with a paid internship received at least one job offer, whereas only 37 percent of those who were not paid received an offer. When it came to salary, the results were even worse. For those who *were* offered jobs, the unpaid interns received less money than those without any internship experience period.

Working for free is not the "opportunity" we often think it is. Opportunity doesn't pay the bills. Exposure won't put food on the table. And working for free sets a bad precedent that's hard to break later. If you want to stop starving, you can't continue doing favors for people and expect it to lead to anything other than bankruptcy.

Imagine if Michelangelo had never charged for his art. Would he have been able to create such a massive body of work, spending most of a century on it? What about Hemingway? If he had written only for the love of his craft, would the world have ever received *The Old Man and the Sea*? It's unlikely. And here we are faced with an important principle, the Rule of Value: the Starving Artist works for free; the Thriving Artist always works for something. As artists, we must value our work before others will.

One of the oldest lies we believe is that if you do something you love and charge for it, the money somehow taints the work. When it comes to other trades, payment is expected; but with writers, photographers, designers, and other artists, we seem to think they don't warrant the same serious treatment that an engineer or carpenter might receive.

Why is this? Part of the blame belongs to the artists themselves. We often go along with the devaluation of our work—we who are prone to self-doubt and insecurity feed the questioning of what value we offer. So when someone asks for a favor, we go along with the request. Real artists don't have to get paid to create, do they? Can't we just do it for the love of it? Maybe not.

When we undervalue our work, we end up playing the martyr, resenting the free gig halfway through the process. "When I notice myself resenting my clients and wanting to quit," Melissa Dinwiddie said, "I realize I don't need to quit. I just need to raise my prices. If you're feeling resentment at all, you're charging too little."

In the years since that first commission, Melissa has transitioned from hobbyist to professional, codifying her approach to charging for her art. "We live in a culture that takes money very seriously," she said. Because we take money seriously, we take seriously the things we pay for. At the same time, income isn't everything. Becoming a Thriving Artist is not just about making a living; it's about setting your work up for success. Money becomes the means to doing more work.

We must, therefore, learn the discipline of charging what we're worth, as Melissa did. When her friend agreed on the sum of twenty-five dollars for that hand-lettered piece, it was a simple exchange, but one that changed everything. And once she started getting paid to create, there was no longer any doubt in her mind about whether or not she was an artist.

Money is part of the process of becoming an artist, if for no other reason than it affirms you are a professional, but the decision to be taken seriously is yours alone. You set the tone for how people will treat you, which means you must believe your work is worth charging for.

ALWAYS WORK FOR SOMETHING

When the prolific science-fiction writer Harlan Ellison was asked to contribute an interview for a film project on the making of the TV show *Babylon 5*, he said, "Absolutely!" There was just one small stipulation: "All you've got to do is pay me."

> ⟫ YOU MUST BELIEVE YOUR WORK ⟪
> ⟫ IS WORTH CHARGING FOR. ⟪

"What?" the young woman on the other end of the call asked, as depicted in a video on YouTube.

"You've got to pay me!" he replied.

"Well," she said, "everyone else is just doing it for nothing."

This was when Ellison, who has a reputation for being a bit gruff, lost it. "By what right would you call me and ask me to work for nothing?" he said. "Do you get a paycheck? Does your boss get a paycheck?"

"Well, yes," she admitted. But, "it would be good publicity."

"Lady," he said calmly, "tell that to someone a little older than you who just fell off the turnip truck."

As a long-time screenwriter, Ellison has seen many come and go in Hollywood. He understands how the business works, what the economics are, and how one can survive in a very competitive market that is often unkind to creatives. He's also seen new writers come to town not understanding that they ought to be paid for their work.

"It's the amateurs," he said, "who make it hard for the professionals."

Ellison has a standard he sticks to: he never works for free. Regardless of what everyone else does, he will not give in to a system that takes advantage of talented people because that's the status quo. And because of this standard, he is one of the most successful writers in Hollywood, having published more than seventeen hundred stories, screenplays, scripts, and essays. Apparently doing the opposite of what everyone else is doing is not always a bad plan.

My suspicion is that charging for his art has less to do with the money and more to do with dignity. It's a matter of taking yourself seriously and seeing others do the same. And nobody knew that better than Michelangelo.

In the spring of 1548, an equally cantankerous artist sent a letter from Rome to his nephew Lionardo in Florence. At seventy-three years old, having sculpted the *David*, painted the Sistine Chapel, and accomplished numerous other creative feats, Michelangelo was disgruntled about a priest's request that he paint an altarpiece. But it wasn't the request itself that offended him; rather, it was the way it was made.

"Tell the priest not to write to me any longer as 'Michelangelo sculptor,'" the aging artist wrote his nephew, "because here I'm known only as Michelangelo Buonarroti, and if a Florentine citizen wants to have an altarpiece painted, he must find himself a painter. I was never a painter or a sculptor like one who keeps a shop. I haven't done so in order to uphold the honor of my father and brothers."

Today, that letter may come across as grumpy, but we have to remember that early in the Renaissance, artists were not honored members of society. They were manual laborers, akin to handymen, and at this time, only nobility or socially prominent individuals had surnames. What we see here are not merely the complaints of an old man but an attitude that was true of Michelangelo his entire life: he refused to be counted among his peers.

Michelangelo's insistence that the priest call him by his last name was a power play. He was not just another hired hand; he was an artist, a title he spent his life redefining. So the clergyman's condescending request made the artist set the record straight. Michelangelo was more than a manual laborer, and the priest's refusal to acknowledge this was an insult. This belief made him, ultimately, the wealthiest artist of his time. His success was due, in part, to how the artist thought differently of himself. Such thinking guided him through life and afforded him opportunities no artist had ever before received.

Don't make a habit of working for free. Without money, you don't get to make more art. Try to always work for something, even if that something is the chance to do work that pays. But be very careful here, because it can be easy to set a bad precedent that you don't value your work. And if you don't, neither will anyone else. So, charging what you're worth begins with the belief that you're worth what you charge.

BECOME YOUR OWN PATRON

But what about the person who wants to create for the sake of creating? "I don't care about the money," he says. "I just want to make my art." Where does this person fit?

> **CHARGING WHAT YOU'RE WORTH BEGINS WITH THE BELIEF THAT YOU'RE WORTH WHAT YOU CHARGE.**

Paul Jarvis worked for corporate clients building websites, which was a decent living but one in which he felt that his creative work was beholden to the whims of other people. Since he was already self-employed as a contractor, he decided to separate himself one more layer from that world of bureaucracy and red tape to launch his own business.

"There wasn't one moment where I was like 'I can't do this,'" he said, but "more like repeatedly, over time, I just kept noticing how far my view of the world and my clients' view of the world differed. I worked for myself, after all, because I wanted my views and beliefs to drive my work instead of profits or shareholders."

Paul started looking more intensely for the type of work and the type of companies and clients that felt good to work with. "It was a gradual shift," he said, "to move away from Fortune 500s and move toward mindful entrepreneurs as clients. I'm fairly sure there wasn't any change to my income either, since I've never dropped my rates. Income stayed the same, but 'the feels' definitely grew. I was happier to work. Not that it was all rainbows and butterflies shooting out of my computer screen at all times. It was still work, but overall, it was more enjoyable, and I didn't mind putting more of me into it."

Today Paul is a designer and writer who in his own words "spends his time at the intersection of creativity and commerce." He sells books and courses based on two decades of experience as a freelancer. He finally stopped waiting to get paid by some corporate benefactor and took his destiny into his own hands. This is the New Renaissance in action. No longer do artists have to be circus performers, playing for peanuts. We can acknowledge what we're worth and demand to be paid. We can become our own patrons, if we learn to charge what we're worth.

Recently I met with Bill Ivey, the former chairman for the National Endowment of the Arts. He told me that we sometimes think the alternative to the Starving Artist is what he calls the Subsidized Artist, but that's the wrong way to think about it. Art needs money. We can deny it all we want and pretend starving makes for better art, but starving often makes for no art at all. Paint costs money. Ink does too. So does food and just about everything else in life. You have to find a way to pay for your art if you want to keep making it.

"I don't think there is any serious evidence," Ivey told me, "that freeing an artist from commercial constraint or other constraints is a direct line to higher-quality work." Still, we drag our feet on this. *If only a patron would come along and pay my bills*, we think. *If only I didn't have to worry about money or business. If only I could just create.* But the responsibility for your getting paid is yours and yours alone. And maybe this is not a bad thing after all.

Creativity and commerce have always coexisted, and these

constraints can create unique opportunities in and of themselves. Financial need can force an artist to hit her deadlines faster. And as much as art needs money, money also needs art. The popes and kings of the world are indebted to artists for preserving their legacies via portraits and tombs and all kinds of art. Art and business have always needed each other and worked together over the years. The world we live in today is the result of such a timeless marriage.

This matter of art and money is not a balancing act, though. It is a dance. Our best work comes from the tension of trying to serve our craft and meet the demands of the market. This is the world we live in. Charles Dickens did some of his best work while serializing his stories to pay the bills. Vincent van Gogh's genius may have emerged from the financial strains that ailed him, but it was his brother's money-mindedness that kept him creating. Money and art: we need them both.

Some artists tend to think making money is either a system you sell out to or something to be avoided altogether. But in reality, it's neither. If you don't make money, you won't have any art to make. We must seek to better understand the business of being an artist. Ignoring this reality is the fastest route to stop creating altogether. To be an artist is to be an entrepreneur. We must learn to embrace this tension and the beauty that comes from it.

"For so long," Paul Jarvis told me, "business has owned art. But now it's the other way around. And I love that." It's not just traditional artists who are redefining the way creative work is considered. It's also writers and actors and designers who are stepping up to acknowledge the value they offer.

To be a Thriving Artist, you have to adopt the mind-set of an entrepreneur. This doesn't mean you have to be greedy, but you can't be naive either. Like Melissa Dinwiddie, you must become comfortable with accepting payment for the effort you put forth. Charging what you're worth isn't just about compensation. It's about dignity—the value you place on your own work and the value other people give it.

When Michelangelo set out to become an artist, he wasn't just chasing a passion—he was trying to reestablish his family name. He needed people to take him seriously. Like the master, we must require the world to do the same, letting go of the myth that artists are not worth their wages.

Your work matters. But the world won't recognize this until you do. You have to avoid the temptation to give all your work away for free, believing it will somehow lead to compensation. It won't. Those opportunities often leave the artist feeling frustrated and bitter. I'm not saying you can't be generous or that you should be arrogant, but there's nothing wrong with seeing the value in your work. In the New Renaissance, art can be business, and business can be art. To believe anything else will leave you feeling stuck, frustrated, and bitter. It's time to stop undervaluing your work and charge what you're worth.

YOUR WORK MATTERS. BUT THE

WORLD

WON'T RECOGNIZE THIS

UNTIL YOU DO.

Chapter 10

OWN YOUR WORK

The Starving Artist sells out to an early bidder. The Thriving Artist owns his work.

No price is too high to pay for the privilege of owning yourself.
—NIETZSCHE

IN THE WINTER OF 1598, FIVE OWNERS OF AN ENGLISH ACTING company stormed the site of the Theatre in Shoreditch, England, just outside of London. They were not there to perform, however; they were there to tear it down. The men belonging to a company called Chamberlain's Men piled several tons of wood on the backs of horses and carried the theater away, piece by piece. Near the river, they used the wood to reassemble the building into what would become the now-famous Globe, home to many Elizabethan plays and performances.

It was a pivotal moment for Chamberlain's Men. On the verge of bankruptcy, they were beholden to a landlord named Giles Allen who wouldn't let them out of their contract. For two years, they had not been performing at the Theatre and were forced to find other means of landing acting gigs. However, the brothers Richard and Cuthbert Burbage, who had inherited the company from their father, had recently discovered a loophole in the agreement: Allen owned the land, but the Burbages owned the building. In an act of desperation to win their independence from the greedy landlord, the brothers reached out to the rest of the acting troupe, offering a 10 percent ownership stake in Chamberlain's Men to anyone who contributed seventy pounds to help relaunch the company across town.

Among the men considering the offer was a young playwright named William Shakespeare.

It was not an easy decision. At the time, Shakespeare was far from famous and was undecided about whether he would keep writing plays. Another option was to become a poet, selling his work to a patron. Of course, he'd have to give up creative control, but he'd have more security. At thirty-four years old, he'd had some success, but seventy pounds was no small investment.

At the time, English playwrights were subject to the demands of their companies and patrons, so when a young artist had the chance to become part owner of an acting company, that was quite the opportunity. Shakespeare must have felt the weight of such a decision: either he could continue on this current path, responsible to landlords and theater owners, or he could head in an entirely new and risky direction. If he joined the new company, the venture could fail and he would be out of a job. But if the playwright stayed where he was, he could miss the chance to be part of something new and exciting, something he could own.

There was risk on both sides, as there always is, but one clearly had a much bigger potential payoff. Shakespeare took the risk and gave up the security of being a freelancer to become an owner, and the following year was one of the most important periods in his career. In 1599 he became the Bard, writing some of his greatest works, including *Much Ado About Nothing*, *Henry V*, and *Julius Caesar*.

And it all began with a decision to buy in to a small but scrappy acting company that allowed him to retain his independence and share in the rewards.

In our own creative careers, we will face similar decisions, and we must remember that our primary job as artists is to make sure we can continue creating our art. Shakespeare understood this when he decided to join the march across town and tear down the Theatre. It was a risk, but it was the kind of risk that gave him the opportunity to potentially own, and therefore control, more of his work. Incidentally, the Globe was the first theater in London to be built and owned by actors. Soon it would become home to many of Shakespeare's plays, making him the household name he is today. None of it would have happened if he hadn't first made that bold transition from artist to owner.

The Rule of Ownership

In 1962 Jim Henson did a series of commercials for Purina Dog Chow and designed a couple of new puppets, one of which became Rowlf the dog. They shot the commercials quickly, and Henson's studio billed the dog food company $1,500 for the cost of building the puppets. At the end of filming, Purina offered Henson $100,000 to buy the rights to Rowlf completely. Agent Bernie Brillstein nearly jumped at the offer, but Henson warned him: "Bernie, never sell anything I own." After the Purina commercials, Jim Henson kept Rowlf, throwing him into a cupboard where he nearly forgot about him until 1976 when the puppet joined the cast of the Muppets. Today Rowlf is undoubtedly worth a lot more than $100,000.

For any creative, the challenge of earning a living is formidable.

We need to sell our work in order to live and eat, but if we sell off everything we create, we can end up starving again. The goal is to not live month to month, but to have enough margin to keep creating. The more you own of your work, the more creative control you have. The Starving Artist sells out to an early bidder, but the Thriving Artist holds out and owns as much of his work as possible.

This is the Rule of Ownership. As creatives, our job is not only to create great works but to protect those works. We must, therefore, resist the temptation to sell out too soon. Settling for a nice payday can lead to short-term success, but it won't buy the kind of legacy we want. We must think long term if we want the kind of freedom that allows us to create what we want while still reaping the rewards of our creation. We all desire a long and prosperous career, one that will hopefully endure after we are gone. The way we ensure the future success of our work is to own the work.

> ## The Starving Artist sells out to an early bidder, but the Thriving Artist owns as much of his work as possible.

In 2003, Jay-Z had proven himself not only as a skilled artist but as a savvy businessman as well, and two major record labels—Universal and Warner Music—were offering him executive positions at their companies. Universal was debating whether to offer him an executive post at their hip-hop label, Def Jam Records.

That fall, the rap artist began having conversations with Universal's CEO, Doug Morris, who liked him because of his entrepreneurial background with his own Rocawear apparel line. Many discussions ensued and in 2004, Universal offered Jay-Z a three-year contract to run Def Jam as the company's president. It was a deal worth between $8 million and $10 million a year, depending on performance bonuses. At the same time, Warner tried to lure him with an even higher salary, including a cut of Warner's upcoming IPO.

The decision was difficult, but Def Jam had one major advantage over Warner: they owned the rights to Jay-Z's master recordings. Under Def Jam's proposed contract, Jay-Z's masters would revert to him within ten years—he would own all his music outright. Despite the offer of less money up front, it was more than enough reason for Jay-Z to accept.

"It's an offer you can't refuse," he said. "I could say to my son or daughter, or my nephews if I never have kids, 'Here's my whole collection of recordings. I own those, they're yours.'" He was starting to think long range, and for the artist who wants to be more than a one-hit wonder, such thinking is essential.

LOSE TO WIN

John Lasseter grew up loving all things Disney—from watching classic cartoons during his childhood in the 1960s to learning in ninth grade he could grow up to become someone who made them. He even attended California Institute for the Arts, a college established by Walt Disney as "a training ground for the next generation of animators."

John spent four years learning how to write, draw, and produce in the Walt Disney way. Everything he did was in preparation for becoming a part of the magical company that had left an indelible impression on him. In 1979 his dream came true when he was hired by the Walt Disney Company as a junior animator to work on the animated film *The Fox and the Hound*. Immediately he was filled with dreams for what the film and company could be. There was just one problem: no one else cared. At the time, the priority of the company was to make profits instead of timeless movies, and they were missing the mark on both.

Not long after his failed attempts to re-envision *The Fox and the Hound*, John pitched a short film idea to his bosses that would leverage the emerging technology of computer animation. He was enthusiastic and motivated about the idea, but again it was summarily dismissed. And then, he was fired. Five years into his dream job, John Lasseter was out of work.

Directionless and disillusioned, he went to work for a small division of Lucasfilm that made hardware and software for high-resolution, computer-generated images. Their flagship product was the $125,000 Pixar Image Computer that had great potential but had found little market success. In fact, the division was hemorrhaging money. Still, the promise of creative fulfillment was irresistible. John was now part of a team of artistic computer scientists who were as obsessed as he was with making a computer-animated movie. But the owner, George Lucas, had been trying to sell the division for years and was convinced the team's quirkiness was a liability. That very quirkiness turned out to be exactly what interested a thirty-one-year-old entrepreneur who wanted to be part of a group that loved art and tech as much as he did. His name was Steve Jobs.

Recently ousted from his own company, Jobs was on the prowl for the next big thing, so he bought the division for $5 million from Lucas, who was in the middle of a divorce and trying to liquidate as many assets as possible. Jobs decided to call the new company Pixar, after the flagship computer the creative team had brought to life.

One of John Lasseter's early encounters with Jobs was to pitch him a story—a computer-animated movie about toys that come to life and have human emotions. It required a $300,000 investment, which was quite the request when Jobs had already invested another $15 million with no foreseeable return. Never one to back down from a challenge, however, Jobs loved the idea. He approved the concept with only one request: "Make it great."

Tin Toy was great, going on to win a 1988 Academy Award for Best Animated Short Film. Shortly after that, Disney reached out to John Lasseter to hire him back for quadruple his previous salary. But he refused. Why work for a place that didn't want what he had to offer? He was finally at the point where he had the kind of creative control he had dreamed of, and he was starting to make the films he'd envisioned when he went to work for Disney.

The Pixar team did, however, accept Disney's money to work on a new project: this time a full-length feature called *Toy Story*. The partnership was complicated, with Disney trying to control too much of what the Pixar team was doing—the story, the dialogue, the character development. They just didn't see things the same way. At one point, when Tom Hanks remarked how mean and sarcastic his character Woody was, John knew the project had to be rescued. During this time, there was a lot of pressure on John and the team. If the project failed, Pixar might be too broke to survive, having already lost $50 million in ten years. But he knew that the work had to speak for itself and so he held his ground on certain creative decisions, eventually convincing Disney to see things his way.

The heart of the movie was restored, and John's vision became a reality.

A week after the premiere of *Toy Story*, the company went public. It was a bold move. After all, who would buy a stake in such an unprofitable company? When their first feature film debuted to unanimously glowing reviews, however, Pixar was valued at twenty-two dollars per share, a valuation that in thirty minutes doubled. Then it reached nearly fifty dollars after an hour, and by the end of the day closed at 800 percent higher than it had started. The company was now worth more than a billion dollars.

John Lasseter didn't want to start an animation company. He wanted to make Disney great again, and he did that by leaving Disney to join Pixar, bringing that studio's storytelling prowess back to the company that had rejected him. In the process, he helped create something worth billions of dollars. It is the classic case of what's at stake when we don't sell out too soon. We must maintain as much ownership of our work as possible, not because it will make us rich but because it will make the work better.

This should be the chief goal of every artist: to make the work great. Sometimes to accomplish this vision, we must make sacrifices, even walk away from great opportunities. We do this not to hoard our gifts but to maintain the control we need to make our work excellent. It's a short-term loss, long-term gain.

NEVER TRUST THE SYSTEM

In the mid-1990s, while he was in college, Stephen Kellogg started making money playing music. After graduation, though, he got a job with an event promoter. He booked events during the day and took care of logistics at night. It was the kind of job that was close enough to music to feel that he had made the right choice but far enough away that he felt like a caged animal. What he wanted was to be onstage; he just didn't know how to get there.

At the encouragement of some coworkers, Stephen started playing open-mic nights. At twenty-four years old, he began booking small shows wherever he could find a venue. This activated something in him. More than promoting other people's work, his dream was to play.

➤ THE CHIEF GOAL OF EVERY ARTIST IS ➤ TO MAKE THE WORK GREAT.

He caught a break playing a show for a college convention, and the exposure led to Stephen booking forty dates at once. Each show paid between $400 and $750 in cash, which was the kind of money that made him believe this dream just might be possible. "If I was breaking even," he recalled, "I was thrilled. I just loved the idea that I got to be with my friends playing a guitar."

The college tour, which he started playing with some friends, evolved into the formation of an official band: Stephen Kellogg and the Sixers. In 2004, the band signed a contract with major label Universal Records.

The group was grateful for their good fortune. Getting a record contract with Universal meant they'd made it, or at least, that's what they thought. Like a lot of musicians, they believed the label would take care of their careers and all they'd have to worry about was making music. Reaching a new level of success, however, brought complications the band wasn't ready to tackle. Perhaps, they thought, they had sold out too soon or in the wrong way; whatever the case, the Sixers soon learned that success doesn't eliminate self-doubt, and it doesn't guarantee a sustained career.

When the Sixers landed their deal, they didn't feel the freedom they had expected—Stephen in particular. Instead, he felt fear.

"They're going to find out I'm only okay," he said, remembering those feelings years later, "and my songs are only okay, and I'm not worth their investment." He was realizing his lifelong dream of playing music for a living and yet the whole time he was afraid it might go away. "I always feel like the bottom is about to drop out," he confessed.

From 2003 to 2012, Stephen toured with the Sixers, recorded seven studio albums, played more than twelve hundred shows, and shared the stage with James Brown. Who would regard these as anything other than successes? Turns out, Stephen himself.

"I didn't feel like I was reaching the next level," he said, recalling the events from his home in New England. I spoke with him on the phone one afternoon when he was supposed to be cleaning the basement. At times, his voice was confident and pure, and at others, it wavered with uncertainty. I could hear the empathy and vulnerability in his voice that must make him a great performer. When he spoke of the feeling that his band was falling apart and there was a "disappointment that you just can't shake off," that feeling lingered with me for some time after hanging up.

At the height of his success, Stephen Kellogg felt that he had lost control of his career. He wanted to create better art but didn't know how to do it. At that point he learned an important truth: while gatekeepers may give you a payday, it always comes with a cost. And for the Sixers, that cost was freedom. "Oh, my goodness, thank you guys so much for this record deal! I hope I don't let you down!" Stephen said, remembering how he humbled himself before the record executives instead of standing up for himself. "I lived that way for years." Sometimes the Big Break can be a big trap.

In 2012, the band arrived at a decision point. Underpaid, overbooked, and exhausted, the band went on hiatus and never returned. "We'd been knocking out a lower-middle-class income for a decade, and I didn't want to crush those friendships. That was a very lonely period of trying to figure out if we'd screwed something up."

WHILE GATEKEEPERS MAY GIVE YOU A PAYDAY, IT ALWAYS COMES WITH A COST. SOMETIMES THE BIG BREAK CAN BE A BIG TRAP.

The story of Stephen Kellogg and the Sixers might be one of the best examples of why artists need to own their work. Had he looked at the careers of other successful artists, Stephen might have seen a theme: when you own your work, you get to call the shots. And when you trust the system fully, there may come a time when the system no longer needs you. "I wish I'd had a mentor," he told me. "I never picked up on the fact that if you want to get somewhere, look at where you're trying to get and start by studying the people who've gotten where you want to go."

It's a common story. The talent that earns us initial success can quickly become obsolete. And as the demands of the market shift, it's easy to get lost in the shuffle if we are not the ones calling the shots. As quickly as some Big Breaks come, they can even more easily go. Stephen Kellogg and the Sixers trusted the system, and the system spit them out.

The question is, did they really need the system?

RISK AND REWARD

In 1979, when George Lucas began work on the sequel to his surprise-blockbuster *Star Wars*, he had a decision to make. He could leverage his newfound favor with 20th Century Fox, the studio that had backed his unlikely space opera, or he could take a risk and reinvest the money he'd just made into the next film. The safe bet was to go with the studio and not gamble on the possibility of a sequel coming close to the success of its predecessor. But Lucas was suspicious of Hollywood and wanted to retain as much control of his work as possible.

In their first deal, Fox had kept 60 percent of the profits of *Star Wars* in exchange for a $10 million investment in a film that was considered a risky endeavor. As one executive put it, "My Lord, we are now going to spend ten million dollars on a film that features something that looks like a giant stuffed animal?" But to everyone's surprise, the film was a runaway success, grossing over $780 million at the worldwide box office, and because of this success, Lucas no longer needed to beg Fox for money. "Okay," he remembered saying, "you took that risk. I'm willing to take the risk on the next one. I'm willing to put up my own money.'"

Lucas invested $20 million of his own money to finance *The Empire Strikes Back* and used his investment as leverage to negotiate a better deal with Fox. In what was nearly the exact opposite of the previous arrangement, he would start at 50 percent of the gross profits and eventually go up to 77, with Fox paying all distribution costs. Fox could release the film to theaters for only seven years; afterward, all rights reverted to Lucas. He would also own all TV rights and earn 90 percent of merchandising profits. Plus, Fox still had to pay him a $10 million advance. Worried that Lucas might take the offer elsewhere, however, the studio begrudgingly signed the deal, and production began. In a matter of a few years, the tables had turned, and now it was Lucas who was in control. When Fox asked the young filmmaker who was going to write, direct, and star in *Empire*, he replied, "None of your business."

When *The Empire Strikes Back* hit the box office, it grossed four times what *Star Wars* did in the opening weekend and would go on to make more than half a billion dollars worldwide, proving to Hollywood and the rest of the world that the film franchise was here to stay. Because George Lucas took the risk, he got the reward, which was something he would do for the rest of his career. With every new film and project, he would continue to gamble on each new creation, sometimes going nearly bankrupt to do so, but always coming out the winner. He would never leave the fate of his creative work up to anyone other than himself.

In the case of *Star Wars*, ownership made Lucas billions of dollars. But it was never about the money. It was always about the work. The success of *Star Wars* allowed Lucas to make *The Empire Strikes Back* on his own terms, and the money he made from the film helped fund the creation of Skywalker Ranch, a place he envisioned as a getaway for filmmakers to dream and create. None of this, however, would have happened had he not fought for control of his work.

This is what ownership does. It gives you options. The Starving Artist tends to trust the system and hope for the best, but that's a bad idea. "The object," Lucas said, "is to try and make the system work for you, instead of against you." The safest place for your work to stay is with you. No one has a more vested interest in your success than you do. Don't trust the system to take care of you; that's not what it was designed to do. Do whatever it takes to own your work; fight to keep the control. Failure to do this will most likely hurt you far more than it will help.

Ownership can be costly in the short term, but it's worth it in the long term. John Lasseter could have made more money going back to work for Disney as an animator, but he would have given up everything he had sacrificed to gain—namely, freedom and control over his work. It wasn't about the money; it was about who controlled the art. To own our work, we may have to take a temporary pay cut or make a short-term sacrifice, but these decisions allow us to do more of the work we want, the way we want to do it. And if you take the risks no one else will take, you'll earn the rewards no one else gets. Someone must own the work, and that someone might as well be you. As the musician Prince once put it, "If you don't own your masters, your master owns you."

OWNERSHIP BUYS FREEDOM

When Stephen Kellogg signed his first record deal, he moved too fast. "I used to want to become Bon Jovi," he said. And who can blame him? Nobody told him how to take the right steps that lead to long-term creative success. So he emulated what he saw and paid the price. But many artists end their careers right there, licking their wounds, without a road map for what to do next. They trusted the system and the system failed them.

Fortunately for Stephen, his story does not end there. On the night of his band's final live performance at Webster Hall in New York City, Stephen was offered a solo record deal, which became his first EP, *Blunderstone Rookery*. Since then, he has been touring extensively, now with a new set of rules, ambitions, and expectations in mind. "I'm looking at what I can become now," he told me. "My whole philosophy with art is to make a living," he said from his home in New England. "We all do our art for different reasons, and I do it because I want to take care of my family. I want to be a guy who can give my kids a good start, and give back."

Now, he does that not beholden to any gatekeeper or system but as an independent musician. He is excited about what's happening for him these days and proud of his most recent record, the first project over which he's had full creative control. Stephen Kellogg is beginning to embrace the New Renaissance. For him, success is "being able to look yourself in the eye and know that you did everything you could to be the highest version of what you think you can be." In the end, being an artist is about creating great work, and ownership is the way we get to ensure that greatness.

George Lucas eventually did give up complete creative control of his company and sold Lucasfilm to Disney for $4 billion. It was an opportunity to take the franchise to a whole new level, one Lucas was unlikely to reach on his own. And this raises an important point: sometimes, it makes sense to sell out. Like John Lasseter, Lucas was obsessed with making the work great, and that sometimes means selling your work to someone who can make it better.

This always ought to be done in the interest of the art, not as an act of desperation. Jim Henson told his agent to never sell anything he created, but by the end of his life he, too, was in talks about an acquisition of the Muppets. We must hold out for as long as we can, being careful not to sell out too soon. It's not that selling out is bad. But selling out in the wrong way, at the wrong time, and for the wrong reasons, is what we need to avoid.

At some point, however, it may make sense to give up some rights to your work and let go of creative control. If such an opportunity earns you the chance to do more of the work with fewer financial constraints, do it. Just remember these occasions are rare and ought to be approached with caution. We should not forget that when we trust others to act in our best interest, we are betting on a system that is not working for us.

If you ever do sell your work to a publisher or record company or investor, do it on your terms and for the right reasons, not because you think it's the only way. In the cases of Lucas, Lasseter, and Henson, selling their companies meant being able to do better work on a larger scale without losing the quality they had spent decades fighting for. We must be wary of accepting early opportunities to sell out, to give up ownership before we know what we're worth. There is almost always something better for those who wait.

IT'S NOT THAT SELLING OUT IS BAD. JUST DON'T SELL OUT TOO SOON.

In 1987, when Cirque du Soleil was invited to perform at an arts festival, the nonprofit group was facing financial problems. The leader Guy Laliberte decided to perform at the festival anyway, and the performance ended up being a hit. Afterward, Columbia Pictures took notice of the performance, reaching out to Laliberte about making a movie about Cirque. The offer sounded intriguing enough to pursue but ended up being too good to be true. When Laliberte realized just how much ownership he would have to give up to get Cirque on the big screen, he pulled out. The experience convinced him his company should transition into the for-profit sector and be privately held so he could have all the freedom he needed to operate the company. Today Laliberte is a billionaire.

We must own our masters or our masters will own us.

In the end, being an artist is about  CREATING great work, and ownership is the way we get to ensure that greatness.

Chapter 11

DIVERSIFY YOUR PORTFOLIO

> THE STARVING ARTIST MASTERS ONE CRAFT.
> THE THRIVING ARTIST MASTERS MANY.

And this I would fight for: the freedom of the mind
to take any direction it wishes, undirected.
—JOHN STEINBECK

IN 1987, MARK FRAUENFELDER READ AN ARTICLE IN AN ISSUE OF THE *Whole Earth Review* about the indie magazine revolution. He thought to himself, *We've got to do a zine ourselves. It would be so much fun.* The next year, he and his wife started *Boing Boing*, a pop culture and technology publication. It launched first in print, then online in 1995. The project was mostly for fun. Mark was a mechanical engineer at the time; when *Boing Boing* launched, he kept his job in the disc drive industry, but the seeds for a creative career were planted.

In 1993, Mark was invited to join the team at *Wired* magazine. As associate editor, he launched their first website and became acquisitions editor for the magazine's book publishing division. He did all this without any formal journalism experience while still doing *Boing Boing* on the side, learning as he went, having fun every step of the way.

In 2005 Mark's curiosity led him to found another magazine called *Make*, which covered technology projects and the growing "maker" movement. Ten years later, he self-published a book about magic tricks. Today he runs many projects, including *Boing Boing*, which is still up and running. In addition to the writing and publishing projects, Mark is also an artist whose work has appeared in exhibitions throughout the United States. He designed the cover art for Billy Idol's record *Cyberpunk*, and has worked on many print ads and other creative projects.

This is how Mark's brain works. He can't stay stuck on one thing for too long. He must move from project to project, idea to idea. "For better or for worse," he said, "I am really interested in a lot of different things, and trying things out myself to see what it's like to actually experience producing media or other things is always interesting."

Often we think a lack of focus is a bad thing, but that's not always the case. Publishing magazines. Writing books. Teaching magic tricks. Designing album artwork for punk rockers. Does this sound like the work of a master artist? It should. Not because Mark does one thing, but because he does many.

The Rule of the Portfolio

When asked the question "What do you do?" most of us tend to answer with a one-word reply. Either that or we stumble over long, complicated responses that leave the person confused. But since when does a single job description define what a person is capable of?

It doesn't.

For the past century, we have been told a story about work that says we must commit to a certain path in life, spend most our career doing that one thing, and not veer too far from our area of focus. This, we think, is what mastery is all about. But is that really what great artists do? Is mastery made of one craft or many?

Your art is never beholden to a single form. You can always change and evolve, and the best artists do this regularly. They understand that in order to thrive, you have to master more than one skill. This is the Rule of the Portfolio: the Starving Artist believes she must master a single skill, whereas the Thriving Artist builds a diverse body of work.

In the Renaissance, people embraced this intersection of different disciplines, and those who blended them best were rightly called "masters." Today, we live in what is called the "gig economy," where jacks-of-all-trades have opportunities to thrive as never before, giving birth to a new kind of worker. Business philosopher Charles Handy called this class of workers who juggle more than one thing at a time "portfolio people" and predicted soon we would all be living these kinds of lives. It seems we are now living in that reality.

"[It is] hard to tell them when people ask me what I do," Mark told me from his home in California. "What I do is just pick one thing, and I'll say, I'm a magazine editor, or a writer, or a blogger. So, yeah, I think I'm just generally a person who will do things that require creativity and communication."

Of course, he does much more than those things, and the fact that he feels a need to explain himself tells us how much we like to pigeonhole people into a single job description. But we don't have to do that. Like Mark, we can develop a rich and diverse portfolio that allows us to do interesting and creative work for a lifetime. In the New Renaissance, our success is contingent on our ability to master multiple crafts. The reason we do this is that it gives us an edge on the competition. Would you rather hire a writer who is only good at crafting prose, or one who also understands marketing? Would you prefer to work for a boss who only knows how to get things done or one who also has emotional intelligence? When we develop a diverse portfolio, we do better and more interesting work.

A DISTRACTIBLE MIND

Starving Artists believe that to make a living you must make money off your art. But Thriving Artists don't just live off their art. Like good investors, they keep diverse portfolios, relying on multiple income streams to make a living. Rarely do they go all in on any single area of work. The challenge, then, is knowing what investments to make and when.

> YOUR ART IS NEVER BEHOLDEN TO A SINGLE FORM. YOU CAN ALWAYS CHANGE AND EVOLVE, AND THE BEST ARTISTS DO THIS REGULARLY.

In 1985 Michael Jackson paid $47.5 million for a music catalog that included 250 songs by the Beatles. At the time, people in the industry thought the deal was crazy. It was such a large sum of money, and the artist was quickly becoming one of the most popular musicians in the world, racking up hit after hit. Why distract himself with investing in another artist's music? It didn't make sense.

But Jackson knew the Beatles catalog was invaluable. What's more, he believed it to be an important piece of history, a cultural artifact worth preserving. It also ended up being a sensible investment. Since Jackson's purchase of the Beatles' catalog, the value of those songs has increased more than 1,000 percent, making it worth more than $0.5 billion.

The acquisition was one of the greatest deals in music business history. Surprisingly, it wasn't initiated by a producer or record company executive but by an artist. The exchange was executed by someone who, in our minds, should have been focusing on his craft. Shouldn't Michael Jackson have been playing music and performing, not orchestrating eight-figure acquisitions? After all, it wasn't even his music. But he was doing just what Thriving Artists do: he wasn't going all in on one big bet. He was diversifying his portfolio.

How did Jackson see the potential in the Beatles catalog when no one else did, and why was he paying attention in the first place? "Predominantly it was his own business sense," said entertainment attorney Donald David, who knew Jackson personally. "I once sat and talked to him for over an hour and he just knew the music business front to back. And he had good instincts. He had really good instincts."

Jackson's instincts told him that it wasn't enough to just sing and perform. He needed to master more than one thing if he wanted to stay in control of his work. And today, thanks to those instincts, Michael Jackson's estate is worth billions. Not bad for a kid who grew up singing rhythm and blues with his brothers.

Creative people tend to live in the world of ideas and possibilities. Because of this, we may struggle with a lack of focus, but this is not always a bad thing. A wandering mind can be an asset if you learn how to use it. To spot the right places to invest your time and resources, you need what Dr. Darya Zabelina calls a "leaky mental filter." A researcher who teaches at Northwestern University,

Dr. Zabelina has discovered a link between creative achievement and the ability to broaden a person's attention. A leaky mental filter is the ability to hold multiple conflicting ideas in tension with each other in a way that they can build upon each other. "People with leaky attention might be able to notice things that others don't notice or see connections between things," she told me, "which might lead to a creative idea or creative thought."

This ability allowed Michael Jackson to see something nobody else saw. It gave Mark Frauenfelder the ability to build a diverse portfolio that allowed him to work on *Boing Boing* and *Wired* at the same time, not to mention countless other projects. Both were competing interests for his time and energy, and both flourished. Under the right circumstances, being distractible can be a strength. "If you think about the most creative people," therapist Chuck Chapman told me, "they're the ones who innovate. They come up with the ideas, and I think the fact that your brain is going so fast all the time and seeing so many possibilities—that's what creates innovation."

Not only does a leaky filter give you insight into possibility; it allows you to identify new opportunities and take advantage of them.

TACKLE NEW SKILLS

In the middle of his life, Michelangelo, now a well-established artist, undertook a new discipline—architecture—and began designing St. Peter's Basilica in Rome. At a time when most people double down on mastering the skills they've already acquired, he learned a new one. He did this at the beginning of his career, too, starting with sculpture, then moving to painting and other crafts as the needs arose. Every decade or so, the artist would tackle a new skill, essentially reinventing himself and adding something new to his ever-increasing portfolio.

And because he did this, he was unbeatable.

Later in life, he oversaw the construction of a major building project that required him to become a foreman. Michelangelo ended up being an excellent organizer of labor, spending decades running huge creative projects as head designer and supervisor. Some of these projects were carried out by more than three hundred assistants, all hired and supervised by the same man who painted the Sistine Chapel.

It is not the singularly focused mind that is able to manage such feats, nor is it the reclusive artist who can manage a team. Rather, it is a *distracted* mind that can bring such energy to tackle a wide array of projects. Michelangelo was more than a sculptor or a painter. One historian went so far as to call him a CEO. But all his skills complemented one another, building on each other and creating a memorable body of work.

How did he do this? He rarely said no to a new skill, at least when it could contribute to his portfolio. If we want to create enduring work and not just a series of one-hit wonders, we, too, must be open to learning new things. The path to a diverse portfolio is not a series of giant leaps but of small steps. One skill sets into motion the need for another, and so on.

In Michelangelo's case, his adeptness at sculpture led to learning architecture, which he didn't attempt until he was forty. These things take time, but the eye for possibility prepares you for such an undertaking. With a superior ability in sculpting, Michelangelo was able to grasp the fundamentals of architecture and translate those lessons to becoming an engineer. In his spare time, he wrote poetry. "There are almost no writer/artists in the world who are both poets and artists," historian William Wallace told me. "Michelangelo is a major poet as well as a major artist. William Blake is one of the others. To have that capacity means you have a brain flexibility that allows you to move between word and image, and that gives you a toolset that gives you a bigger range of vocabulary than some of the rest of us."

This is the leaky filter in action. Michelangelo acquired the skills he needed, which allowed him to spend the greater part of a century creating. He was not above learning something new and was adept at taking it all in, then focusing on the right thing at the right time. You build a diverse body of work by embracing different interests, then using your leaky filter to explore opportunities and add new skills to the portfolio when needed. Michael Jackson's openness to identify business opportunities and a willingness to grow in new areas allowed him to not only make a profitable investment but also secure a cultural heirloom.

Starving Artists try to master one skill. Thriving Artists acquire whatever skills necessary to get the job done. One is about short-term rewards; the other is about creating for a lifetime. If you don't believe the myth that mastery is just doing one thing, then you, too, can create a body of work that will endure.

DIVERSITY PAYS

In 1992 a twenty-seven-year-old rapper named Andre Young, AKA Dr. Dre, started Death Row Records with his partner, Suge Knight. The new label was launched just after Dre's exit from NWA, the hip-hop group that had launched his career. It was a risky move to walk away, but this was the kind of thing that would allow Dre to succeed in ways no other rapper had.

Death Row began with $250,000 of start-up capital. Less than a year after forming the company, the two partners signed a $10 million deal with Interscope Records to distribute their records. They had been acquiring artists such as Snoop Dogg, Tupac Shakur, and MC Hammer, all who went on to become enormously successful. The label retained all publishing and recording rights. By 1996 the company was making more than $100 million a year.

STARVING ARTISTS TRY TO MASTER ONE SKILL. THRIVING ARTISTS ACQUIRE WHATEVER SKILLS NECESSARY TO GET THE JOB DONE.

Four years after cofounding the label, Dr. Dre was unhappy with the direction of the company and his partner, who was becoming increasingly dangerous. Suge once negotiated a business deal on Dre's behalf with a baseball bat. Despite the success they were experiencing, Dr. Dre decided to walk away from Death Row, leaving behind a 50 percent stake in the company. He not only gave up all rights to the company, he also lost his own recordings as an artist. Once again, he was on to the next thing: a new label he called Aftermath Entertainment.

At Aftermath, Dre attracted new talent, including rappers Eminem and 50 Cent, helping launch their careers to incredible stardom. Death Row was eventually sold off for $18 million, a far cry from the $100 million it had been bringing in. Dre's instincts were right. Moving on, no matter how costly, was the right call. As we've seen, there are benefits to not getting pigeonholed into one thing. Throughout his career, Dr. Dre would continue to branch out into new ventures, acquiring various skills as he went. And as he did, he began to see new possibilities for his art and business.

In 2006 Dre met with friend and music producer Jimmy Iovine. Iovine was concerned with two problems currently facing the music industry. The first was how piracy was affecting record sales, and the second was the prevalence of low-quality audio due to Apple's plastic earbuds. Apple, Iovine said, was selling "$400 iPods with $1 earbuds." Dre responded with a similar amount of frustration. "Man, it's one thing that people steal my music," he said. "It's another thing to destroy the feeling of what I've worked on."

Iovine and Dre decided to do something about it, and together they created the headphone company Beats, of which Dr. Dre is the main representative. Of course, Dre is not just the face of Beats—or of anything he does. He is the producer, the linchpin, the man making it all happen. It started with helping launch NWA, which brought attention to the West Coast hip-hop scene. Then, he founded not one but two successful record labels that launched the careers of countless artists. And with Beats, he was involved not just in the design of the product but in running the business as well. "I've been living the American Dream for over twenty-five years," he said in an interview, "just being able to do what I do, be creative and make money out of it, it's incredible."

Until recently, many professional musicians could only make money off a few income streams, which at most included live events, record sales, royalties from licensing, and merchandise. For some, there weren't even that many, as in the case of songwriters relying primarily on income from songs. Today things have changed. The digital music revolution brought with it some challenges, but it also introduced new possibilities. Now we have the chance to expand our portfolios of work into successful careers. But we must be willing to do what Dr. Dre did and seek them out.

Dr. Dre eventually sold off Beats to Apple in 2014 for $620 million. The deal made Dre one of the wealthiest musicians alive, but it also taught him an important lesson. He had left so many things behind for the sake of something new, and at times, it looked like artistic flakiness. But it was more than that. What Dre was doing was not just bouncing from one creative project to the next. He was building a portfolio.

Today his old partner Suge Knight is in prison, and Dr. Dre is a billionaire.

This is how you build a body of work. You seek out new opportunities and skills, developing a leaky filter to take it all in, and then focus on the skills needed to do the work. In the end, it's about the work, and for Dre, that's not just making music. It's embracing any opportunity to create something new and interesting and helpful. Like any Thriving Artist, he does a lot of things, and that ability to master multiple disciplines has made him very successful. After all, it was his curiosity that drove him to keep creating and searching, even when it meant leaving behind work he had spent years creating. Still, he understood that his best work lay ahead of him, not behind. The same is true for you.

FOCUS ON THE BIG PICTURE

There comes a time to not let your mind wander, to dig in and focus. When you learn to lock in on the larger ideas and let the rest fall to the wayside, you begin to think more about the body of work you are creating than about a single creation. Cultivating a portfolio mindset will keep you focused on what really matters: not on any single work but on the whole creative life itself. How, then, do we take a wandering mind and turn it into a diverse set of interests and skills that can become a body of work?

Being distractible can be a strength in creative work. When we understand that an open mind can guide us into new possibilities, we don't have to try to change ourselves into being more organized or "responsible." Instead, we can use our creative quirks to our advantage, helping us identify opportunities to do fulfilling work that we would have otherwise missed.

BEING DISTRACTIBLE CAN BE A STRENGTH IN CREATIVE WORK.

We must also practice using our leaky filters to find new skills, then learn and apply them. The goal is to use anything that will help you develop a more substantial portfolio, which can lead to a lifetime of creation. And we must keep focusing on the big picture, remembering that what matters more than a single creation or two is building for ourselves a flourishing creative life. Just as smart investors build diverse portfolios, Thriving Artists create a body of work that makes them proud.

"The negative," Mark Frauenfelder told me, "is that you tend to get spread out a little too thin and maybe you don't master certain things as well as other people who are obsessively focused on something. I wouldn't necessarily recommend being a jack-of-all-trades. But I think it's worked for me, and I'm happy living a life of exploring different ways to be creative and try to make a living at the same time."

In his career, Mark has had many different jobs, from working in start-ups to participating in conferences and innovation labs. And it all began with an open mind and a willingness to try new things.

Of course, juggling so many things can be difficult, and there are real costs to a life filled with diverse interests, but when you understand this is not an event but a process, the work becomes richer. When we focus on the big picture, we create for ourselves and the world a portfolio worth noticing and remembering.

Chapter 12

MAKE MONEY TO MAKE ART

The Starving Artist despises the need for money. The Thriving Artist makes money to make art.

*The writer must earn money in order to be able
to live and to write, but he must by no means live
and write for the purpose of making money.*
—KARL MARX

IN LATE 2015 THE APPAREL COMPANY OLD NAVY RELEASED A SERIES of children's T-shirts with "Young Aspiring Artist" written on them but then had the word "Artist" crossed out and replaced with "President" and "Astronaut." Many took offense and went to the Internet to broadcast their discontent. One person on Twitter said: "My high school guidance counselor must of [sic] gotten a job at #old-navy because she told me an artist wasn't a career!"

Old Navy publicly apologized and discontinued the shirts, but the question of whether art is a serious career remains. The admonition to not become an artist and choose a safer path may be politically incorrect, but it is still the way many of us think. In fact, it's an admonition artists often tell themselves—the kind of negative self-talk that has sabotaged entire careers. But is it true that being an astronaut is a safer choice than being an artist?

It wasn't for Alan Bean.

As a boy, Alan's dream was to become a navy pilot, a path he followed with discipline, becoming an aeronautical engineer, then going on to flight training to realize his dream. At this point in life, Alan thought to himself, *This is as good as it gets.*

"I thought I had the best job in the world," he later recalled. But for some reason, it wasn't enough. He kept looking around at the beautiful things in the world and being captivated by them. He saw his neighbors buy some paintings and thought he could probably paint something that looked just as good.

Alan enrolled in night school to take classes in drawing and water coloring. He wasn't any good at first, but he liked it. Many of his navy friends noticed his new hobby and with some concern told him that if he wanted to advance his career, he was better off learning golf. In the close quarters of the military, his affinity for art might arouse some suspicion, but none of that mattered to Alan. He had always done what was interesting to him, so he kept on painting.

The navy pilot's career transitioned into an opportunity to work for NASA, where he was even busier than before. When he could find the time, he continued to take art classes from local teachers in the community. Art was his one and only hobby, and he dedicated himself to it with the same discipline that he gave the rest of his career, albeit in smaller doses.

When he was thirty-seven years old, Alan served as the lunar module pilot for Apollo 12, the second mission to the moon. In November 1969, he became the fourth man to walk on the moon, exploring the lunar surface and installing the first nuclear power generator station there. In 1973, he flew on the space station Skylab 3 as the spacecraft commander for fifty-nine days in orbit. During that time of navigating the cosmos, Alan saw incredible things, things that most people will never get the opportunity to see. One day, while training to fly the space shuttle, he said to himself, "Boy, there's young men and women around here who can do this as good as I can, but there's no one who's been given this gift of walking on the moon."

It gave him pause.

In Alan's mind, anyone could fly the space shuttle, maybe even fly it to the moon. But who else could paint it? It might have been an excess of modesty on his part—astronauts aren't exactly common— but Alan knew he had a gift that needed to be shared. "If I could leave here," he said, "and if I could learn to be better, then I could leave stories and images that wouldn't be done otherwise." As he contemplated leaving NASA, the middle-aged astronaut began to count the cost. He'd been given an incredible education and training to become an astronaut, but he'd also been given the gift of art. "You know, I got to thinking," he said, "it would be nice if Columbus had taken an artist with him. We'd know a lot more. If Magellan had, that would have been a good thing."

Seeing the moon up close and personal, trudging through the dust beneath his feet—these were experiences no other artist could fully express. No one except Alan. And the more he thought about this, the more excited he became. Soon, the choice was obvious: Alan had to paint the moon, and he had to leave NASA to do it. That's how Alan Bean became the first astronaut artist and the only person in history to paint the moon from firsthand experience.

DOING YOUR DUTY

When he left NASA in 1981 to paint full-time, the reaction from Alan's friends was mixed. "About half thought it was a good idea," he said. "The other thought I was having a midlife crisis. And they'd say things to me like, 'Well, look Alan, you've got millions and millions of dollars' worth of training that other people don't have. You think this is a good way to put it to use?' I'd been given this gift, all this training, all this knowledge that I had. It was unusual."

But he had considered that already, and this was more than some creative whim. "I'm a guy who has done his duty his whole life," Alan said. "And, so, I said, 'This is what I should be doing, because they won't miss me here. And if I don't do this, then a lot of these images and a lot of the stories that I captured will be forgotten.'"

Typically, we don't think of art as a duty. If anything, it's an indulgence, certainly not a serious career choice as the Old Navy commercial suggested. But is this true? The urge to be creative is one thing, but the call to be an artist is something else. Clearly, Alan Bean considers his work to be the latter. When he finally did resign at fifty years old, Alan was not merely chasing a passion—he was answering a calling.

"I didn't leave my job as an astronaut because I had this creative urge," he told me, his Texas drawl coming through the phone connection. "I left because I felt it was my duty to do these paintings to celebrate this great event I was blessed to be a part of."

So, here Alan was with this responsibility to paint the moon, something only he could do, and as he began, he realized something. He wasn't that good. "I took my work down and compared it to what was in the galleries and what was in the museums," he said, "and I could see that I wasn't anywhere near there, and I never would be probably as good as what you see. But I could get better and maybe I could get competitive. Because . . . if I was going to devote my life to it, I somehow had to make a living doing it."

He devoted his life to painting. And for more than three decades, his art has allowed him more than enough to live. Today Alan Bean's artwork is featured in galleries all over the United States, with his paintings selling for tens of thousands of dollars apiece, sometimes more. An original called *First Men: Neil Armstrong*, a forty-by-thirty-inch textured acrylic, recently sold for $228,600.

He did his duty, and he did it well.

But the money was never the point for Alan. For this astronaut-artist, his work is a duty, and to do that duty well, he needs to make a living. He makes money so that he can make art, not the other way around. The point is to share his gift, that thing only he can offer the world. Without the money, though, the art would be much harder to make. And so Alan understands something every Starving Artist must grapple with: money is the means to making art, but it must never be the master.

THE RULE OF THE GIFT

When it comes to creative work, there exist two economies. The first is the market economy, that familiar place where goods and services are sold based on their usefulness to us, the consumers. Any modern nation in the past hundred years or so has embraced this as the dominant economic model. And, of course, it is responsible for many wonderful advancements and innovations in society. But it has its limitations as well.

> **MONEY IS THE MEANS TO MAKING ART, BUT IT MUST NEVER BE THE MASTER.**

The second economy is what Lewis Hyde calls the gift exchange economy, which he argues is the place where creativity tends to thrive.

"The essential commerce of the creative spirit is a gift exchange economy," he said. Art, he argues, is a gift, not a commodity. It is not a good you create and hope to get paid for—that's not how it has worked for most of human history, anyway. For thousands of years, the primary model for art-making was a gift exchange one. Only recently did we start thinking art was something we could charge money for.

In 1983, Lewis Hyde published a book called *The Gift*, which has since become a modern classic and underground bestseller among creatives. The book explains why many modern artists struggle to make a living off their work: art is a gift, and since we now live in a market economy, there is going to be a disconnect. In the market, people don't pay for gifts; they pay for commodities. So you must find a way to get paid for the art.

There are three ways to do this. First is that path of the commercial artist in which you sell your art directly to the market. "It's a wonderful day when an artist can do their work and make money off of it," Hyde told me. This is not impossible, but it is far from the norm.

Second is the traditional patronage model where a wealthy benefactor is willing to pay for your livelihood as you do your work. Again, this is a rare occasion and not something to count on.

Third is the path of self-patronage in which you find a way to support the work yourself. "The most common solution to the disconnect between art and commerce," Hyde explained, "is to get a second job. And for most artists, the second job is teaching your own art."

There is, of course, a fourth solution in which the artist chooses poverty and creates from a place of struggle and strife. But this is the least favorable option and far from the wisest. "I have no interest in starving artists," Hyde told me. "I think artists should be well fed. I think artists should be as well paid as doctors and lawyers." But this is not the world we live in. Every artist must fight for margin to create.

For years Professor Hyde followed his own advice and taught writing at Harvard. As time went on, though, he began to consider what was important to him. With a nice base salary and health insurance at his job, he wondered if he could make some small sacrifices to spend more time working on other projects. "There are many moments like that as we go through life," he said, "of trying to figure out, 'Is this necessary?' And if it isn't, what gets freed up if I stop doing it?"

Professor Hyde decided that his writing was necessary, so in the mid-1990s, he cut his teaching time in half. The move to half-time employment gave him the margin he needed while still providing some stability. After the professor made the move, however, he never looked back. "The time was more important to me than the money," he told me, explaining how he justified earning half his previous salary and still being able to live.

When the National Endowment of the Arts had literature grants, it published a collection of stories by recipients of the grants called *Buying Time*. "The idea," according to former NEA chairman Bill Ivey, "was that the NEA, by giving the writer money, just gave them the freedom, the time, to write these great things." That's what Lewis Hyde was doing when he went part-time as a professor: he was buying time.

Creative work is a costly endeavor, both in time and resources, calling us to dedicate large amounts of our lives to it without any immediate reward. When we find ways to make money, it buys us time and gives us the opportunity to create more. This was why Michelangelo never stopped working long after he'd made enough to retire. Income wasn't the goal—continuing to create was. We don't make art for the money. We make money so that we can make more art.

This was the mind-set of Alan Bean and those like him. The Starving Artist despises the need for money, but the Thriving Artist uses money to make more art.

When I asked Lewis Hyde what his outlook on the future of art was, he said, "I think it's neither bright nor dim. Art will always be with us. I believe that young people coming up may take ten years to find out if they can do that work and make a living at it and find an audience. There's an in-between period of trying to get established, and during that period, young artists need support from their communities and need to have communities where they can lead dignified lives without becoming poor."

WE MUST BE CREATING WITH FULL BELLIES AND FULL SOULS.

This is the Rule of the Gift, which says that if art is your duty, then you must create. The nature of a gift is that it is to be given away, so the first duty of an artist is to do your work. There is a spirit of generosity in every creative act, but to embody this generosity we cannot starve. We must be creating with full bellies and full souls, and so the second duty of an artist is to make money to make art.

MONEY MAKES ART

In the 1930s the streets of Japanese cities were overtaken by a group of artists who sold candy and performed picture-based plays for children. At the height of this phenomenon, there were twenty-five hundred vendors, or *kamishibaiya*, in Tokyo alone who performed ten times per day for audiences of as many as thirty children, totaling more than a million a day.

For artists who might otherwise be unemployed in a depressed economy, it was an incredible opportunity. This mobile, candy-selling form of theater was called *kamishibai*, translated as "street theater using painted illustrations."

The artists would travel from town to town by bike with a miniature stage mounted on their backs, announcing the start of a show by banging together two wooden sticks on a street corner and shouting, "*Kamishibai! Kamishibai!*" The children would come running, and if they had money with them, they could buy candy off the back of the bike and get a front-row seat for the show. The storytellers made a living selling candy, and they made art with the pictures they drew for the stories.

The creation of the storyboards was a business, with dealers commissioning and renting artwork to the storytellers for a fee. Some *kamishibaiya* created their own art, while others used the dealers. Illustrators would sketch the drawings first in pencil and then go over them with thick brushes, using India ink. Then they'd apply watercolor paint to delineate the background and foreground and brush tempura paint on top. Last, they'd add a coat of lacquer, which provided a shine that also protected it from the weather.

In *kamishibai* art, the characters featured oversized eyes and light-and-dark contrasts—an approach meant to draw children into the story even if they were seated at the back. A *kamishibai* show included three stories, each of which were approximately ten minutes long. The storytellers would dramatically reenact the scenes while one of the pictures was featured in the frame on the stage.

As the story progressed, the storyteller would remove one picture and reveal the next. The last of the three stories would end with a cliffhanger so the children would want to return the next day. This form of Japanese street theater disappeared with the advent of the television in 1952, but its storytellers endured, as did the art form itself.

The artists went on to spread a new form of art called "manga," which now makes up a global, billion-dollar industry. Today street artists at festivals and fairs are reviving *kamishibai* as an art form. It endures in its own style and in the world of comics and animation.

Walt Disney said, "I don't make pictures just to make money. I make money to make more pictures." This is what most of us want: not to get rich off our creations but to have enough time and freedom to create what we want. We want to have the means to focus on what matters to us.

When I first launched out on my own as a full-time writer, I knew that it would be difficult to make a living writing books. I had friends who were authors, and they told me their horror stories. To make ends meet, I started teaching my craft, as Lewis Hyde said, and what I ended up with was an online business that gave me the freedom and flexibility I needed to write without any pressure to compromise my values for a paycheck. And to this day, this is a model I cling to.

Your art can help you build the kind of life you want, and you don't need to deliver pizzas to do it. For the *kamishibaiya*, the candy sales made the art possible. Without the money, there would have been no art and no audience. The business made the creative side possible; not to mention, it launched an entirely new genre that continues today.

Use What You Have

When Alan Bean began painting for a living, he had an idea to use the tools from his time on the moon in his art—to repurpose the ordinary, everyday tools from his day job and use them in his creations.

"I used the same materials that other artists have used forever, ends of brushes, fingers, pallet knives, you name it. And one day I said, 'Why am I doing this earth technique? I've got the hammer I used on the moon. I've got the core two-bit I drove into the surface. I've got these training moon boots over here. I could make texture using my moon boots, my hammer, and my core two-bit, and it would be space related.'"

And today, these techniques are what make Alan Bean's paintings so valuable. "People love it," he said. "I love it." What he found was a way to do his duty—to paint the moon—and get paid to do it well. Did he do this by simply creating his art and hoping to get paid? Not at all. He danced with the market, meeting the needs of his customers while at the same time satisfying his own sense of what's right.

"You know," he went on, "back long ago when I was on the moon down two meters, I was supposed to throw the little bit away and put a cap on so the dirt wouldn't fall out on the way home. But for some reason I put it in my pocket." That little tool has become one of his instruments for making art.

The paintings are unique—a blend of painting and sculpture that is impossible to replicate. He uses tools from the historic moon landing, including a NASA shovel and his own moon boots to add texture. Early in his career, Alan started adding moon dust from his astronaut suit to make his works even more original, a move he admits was great for marketing.

"I'd get the texture on there," he explained, "and it'd look good to me. I'd think, *Boy, these moon boots look good. Those hammer marks look good.* That idea of texture in my opinion is one of the best ideas I've ever had in art, because it's so different than anybody else's stuff."

Alan didn't try to play by the old rules of an antiquated system that would reject him. He made his own rules, borrowing from what was around him. He followed the rules of the Thriving Artist, embracing his own misfit identity and using tenacity to guide him toward success. And he found a way.

There's always a way for the person who is tenacious enough to find one. You just have to search for one and diligently treat your art as more than a frill, as a duty. You must give away your gift to the world—neither settling for what is expected of you nor starving for your art, but always pushing the boundaries of what is possible.

Yes, you must make money to make art. But don't give income too much importance. Just give it its proper place. We need money to keep the lights on and buy supplies, but it's not everything. As novelist Steven Pressfield wrote, "Money exists, in my world, to buy me another season." Every season you create instead of scramble to find work is a win, and with time, those seasons add up. The more money you have, the more time you have; and the more time you have, the more art you can make.

In our world today, the opportunities to do creative work that both pays the bills and gets noticed are unprecedented. With access to tools and technology we've never had, this is truly the best time to be an artist. To ignore this opportunity is to do a disservice to the work of those who came before us and paved the way. As long as we leverage these tools in ways that do not compromise our character, we honor their legacy and join them in ushering in a New Renaissance.

JOIN THE NEW RENAISSANCE

Against the ruin of the world, there is only
one defense—the creative act.
—KENNETH REXROTH

IN 1909, THE ITALIAN ARTIST AMEDEO MODIGLIANI IS SAID TO HAVE exhibited some sculptures in the charming Tuscan city of Livorno, located on the northwestern coast of the peninsula. According to local legend, citizens of the seaside town criticized the statues, claiming they were so bad that the artist should throw them into the Medici Canal.

As the story goes, that's just what he did. Seventy-six years later, on the one hundredth anniversary of Modigliani's birth, the city of Livorno was preparing for an exhibition to celebrate the artist's work. The hope was that the exhibition would attract tourists and boost the local economy. But when the festivities did not go as planned, with few people turning out and little publicity coverage of the events, the city council commissioned a search of the canals to find Modigliani's lost sculptures.

The search was led by Vera Durbé, curator of the local civic museum and organizer of the exhibition. It cost the city thirty-five thousand dollars. After eight days, the first carving was found on July 24 at nine o'clock in the morning. Eight hours later, a second granite bust was discovered at the bottom of the canal. On August 9, a third was collected, this one slightly smaller than the others. All three busts matched Modigliani's unique style. Durbé wept when she saw them. After a hundred years, the city of Livorno had finally found their legendary lost statues.

When this happened in 1984, the art community was thrown into an uproar. Such a discovery attracted both critics and connoisseurs, all curious to see if the busts were authentic. One critic named Cesare Brandi said it was a "very important" find and "certainly Modigliani's." The director of the French Academy in Rome called them "a resurrection." The curator of the Modern Art Gallery of Rome declared the works were unquestionably original.

Livorno was subsequently overtaken by news media, tourists, and art critics, all who came to underscore the importance of the discovery. Almost all the experts agreed: these were, in fact, the lost statues of Modigliani. Only one historian, Federico Zeri, was bold enough to say the sculptures looked too "immature" to be authentic and suggested that if the great artist had thrown them into the canal, then he was right to do so.

It was around this time, as the small port city began attracting international attention, that three university students—Pietro Luridiana, Michele Ghelarducci, and Pierfrancesco Ferrucci—came forward to confess. The whole thing had been a ruse. As a practical joke, they had fabricated one of the busts in their backyard with a drill and thrown it into the canal.

When they came forward, no one believed their confession. The students provided pictures of the prank to prove their story. The project took about two hours from start to finish, and they had documented the whole process. Even then, there were those who had continued to doubt their claims. On national television, the three students demonstrated with a Black and Decker drill exactly how they had carved the statues.

Another local artist named Angelo Froglia came forward to claim authorship of the other two heads. Some still insisted the works were authentic, citing numerous scientific tests that had proven the legitimacy of the busts. Many professional art critics had staked their professional reputations on the authenticity of these statues, and now a few college students were making them look like fools. Six weeks after the fact, the town of Livorno finally accepted the truth: if Modigliani did throw his rejected statue heads into the canal, they remain undiscovered.

A BEAUTIFUL LIE

The story of the fake Modiglianis illustrates an important human trait. Often, in spite of the evidence, we are more comfortable with tradition than truth. Today those fake heads of Livorno are celebrated not as lost works of art but as part of the city's cultural heritage. "That's how bad it is," said Rab Hatfield, the professor who helped discover the reality of Michelangelo's wealth. When I asked him why people struggle to change their minds about certain ideas like the Myth of the Starving Artist, this was the story he told me. "That's how people are," he concluded.

We often live out the stories we've been told, sometimes without questioning the truthfulness of them. "I am convinced that the three sculptures attributed to Modigliani are all false, just like the ones the boys executed today," said art critic Mario Spagbol in regard to the prank performed in Livorno. "I consider their sculpture today obviously false but also the most beautiful."

False, but beautiful. Perhaps the same can be said for the Story of the Starving Artist. We are used to seeing artists struggle and suffer for their art. This may be an attractive story if for no other reason than it is the most familiar. After all, we have heard this narrative told over and over again. Because it is familiar, we may be tempted to accept it. "People hang on to things that they're accustomed to," Professor Hatfield told me. Sometimes, it's easier to believe a beautiful lie than a difficult truth.

But not always. As we have seen in this book, throughout history there have always been daring individuals who were unwilling to accept the false depiction of an artist as poor and suffering. Instead, they chose a different route: the Path of the Thriving Artist. And when we compare the Myth of the Starving Artist to the model of Michelangelo, we are faced with an entirely new paradigm.

You don't have to starve. Today there is a New Renaissance changing everything we thought we knew about creative work—one that is turning Starving Artists into Thriving Artists—and all we have to do is embrace it. We can, in fact, create work that matters and earn a living doing so. We can share our gift with the world without having to suffer for it. And the sooner we acknowledge this opportunity, the sooner we can get on with doing our work.

A DIFFICULT TRUTH

In the same way Livorno didn't believe their treasured piece of art was a fake, the world may be slow to accept the new truth that real artists don't starve. It's difficult to change an entire society's perspective overnight, but there is one mind you can change today, and that's your own. This was the challenge Michelangelo faced in his own time.

In the Renaissance, artists were not aristocrats as Michelangelo hoped to become. But he was committed to not only making a living but earning the respect of his peers. It was not easy, but in the end, he changed the game for artists. How did he do this?

THERE IS A NEW RENAISSANCE THAT IS TURNING STARVING ARTISTS INTO THRIVING ARTISTS. ALL WE HAVE TO DO IS EMBRACE IT.

First, he mastered his mind-set. When many artists were opening shops to train apprentices, he resisted such temptations to conform. He knew that to make a name for himself, he would have to be different. And before he acted differently, he would have to think differently. He befriended those in power so he didn't have to beg for scraps. He became an apprentice.

Then he mastered the market, plugging into a web of influential relationships that included popes, kings, and patrons who helped his work thrive. Building this network ensured he'd never starve.

Finally, he mastered his money, earning ten times what an average artist made by charging what he was worth. He invested in land and property, which secured his position as an aristocrat. Only the wealthy owned property. But long after he had more than enough money, he kept creating, living twice as long as the average person and creating an unforgettable legacy. He made money to make more art.

"Few artists have achieved as much as Michelangelo," wrote William Wallace, "few so completely embody the notion of artistic genius. . . . More than any of his contemporaries, he significantly raised the stature of his profession, from craftsman to genius, from artisan to gentleman. He demanded respect from his patrons, and he earned prestige as an artist. The era of the superstar artist was dawning."

The age of the Starving Artist is over. The era of the Thriving Artist is upon us. It's time to let go of our assumptions about artists and embrace the New Renaissance. It's time to believe creative work is worth its reward. It's time to thrive.

The point is not to make a fortune or become famous, but to do the work. We are all looking for a way to share our gift with the world without worrying about making a living. That means more than getting paid once for our creations. It means building a life that allows us to keep creating.

To do this, we have to leave behind our notions that artists must suffer. The Picassos and Twyla Tharps of the world didn't do this. They discarded the Myth of the Starving Artist, choosing instead to embrace a new paradigm. We must follow in their footsteps, accepting the importance of networks and relationships in creative work. We must seek patrons and join our scenes if we want to thrive. We must not only make art, but we must also make money.

That is the point—to keep making things. The success is the means, and the end is not having to quit. You don't have to be rich to do that, but you can't starve. That's not how your best work is going to be made.

In this book we've explored how a New Renaissance is not only possible—it's here. We only need to recognize it. If our work is going to thrive, we need to embrace the new rules of what it means to be an artist. Like Adrian Cardenas, we must reimagine what we think is possible for a creative career. We must become apprentices, as Tia Link did, humbling ourselves so that we can eventually become masters. We must be wary of our stubbornness and use our grit to conquer the challenges we face. We must win over patrons and build networks and learn the discipline of charging for our work. Like Stephanie Halligan, we must not be afraid to share our work. We must steal from our influences as Jim Henson did and make money to make art. These Thriving Artists offer a challenge to our own bodies of work. Will we embrace these new rules or reject them?

Not long ago we embraced the story of the Starving Artist as fact, but today we have a better story: real artists don't starve. Now we can join a growing group of creatives who are ushering in a new creative age. We can become Thriving Artists—not amateurs who dream of "making it" someday, but true professionals. Whether your craft is cabinet-making, painting, or business, the world needs your work.

But now you have a choice. You can go the way of the tired, frustrated artist who struggles to keep creating. Or you can embrace an important but challenging truth that just might set you free from such thinking. You don't have to starve. You can thrive. The world is waiting for you to create your best work. Please don't let us down.

Not long ago we

EMBRACED

the story of the Starving Artist
as fact, but today we
have a better story: real
artists don't starve.

Dear Reader,

Thank you for going on this journey with me. If this book has stoked something in you, please send a note to jeff@goinswriter.com. I would love to hear from you. For more resources, including free access to full interview audio and transcripts, along with bonus case studies and other tools, visit dontstarve.com.

Thank you,

Jeff Goins

Acknowledgments

MANY THANKS TO MY FRIEND JOE BUNTING FOR BEING THE FIRST person to enlighten me about the true story behind Michelangelo's wealth. Without his sending me that article, none of this would have happened. (Oh, and Joe—you were right about the title.)

A big thanks to my wife, Ashley, who is endlessly patient with my ridiculousness when I am writing a book (which is most of the time). Also to my in-laws, Pat and Pam: thank you for your support and encouragement.

I am always grateful to my parents for encouraging me in creative outlets—to my mom, Robin, for making me take art classes that didn't go anywhere necessarily productive but left in me an endless fascination with the subject, and to my dad, Keith, who is the best songwriter I know.

Also thanks to my agent, Steve Hanselman, who helped me understand that this book was not about being creative but about being a creative person. And to Ryan Holiday, who helped me with the title, the overall concept, and the writing of the book.

I'm grateful to Chantel Hamilton who served as both my research assistant and editor for the project. If you're in need of a good editor, look her up.

Acknowledgments

Many thanks to the fine folks at Thomas Nelson and HarperCollins who helped turned all these scribblings into a real book: Jenny Baumgartner, Janene MacIvor, and Brian Hampton.

Thank you, as well, to those who put up with my self-doubt about every aspect of this process and gave me feedback as I went: Joel Miller, Tim Grahl, David Molnar, Bryan Harris, Grant Baldwin, Keith Jennings, and Seth Godin.

And lastly, special thanks to Cassia Cogger who served as my final beta reader before I sent this thing out into the world.

Sources

THE PRIMARY RESEARCH BEHIND *Real Artists Don't Starve* WAS THE result of hundreds of surveys and dozens of interviews I collected from professional artists, entrepreneurs, writers, and creatives from a variety of disciplines. In addition, I personally interviewed leading experts, researchers, and academics on the subjects of creativity and business. I also read close to a hundred different biographies, books, articles, and research papers. Below is a bibliographic essay with selected sources, but if you would like a list of all my sources, including free downloads to full interview transcript and audio files, visit dontstarve.com/tools.

INTRODUCTION

The story of Michelangelo's wealth has been covered by a variety of publications. I first stumbled across it in an article by the *Telegraph* and read several articles and interviews on the subject, including a wonderful piece by Frank Bruni in the *New York Times*. The most authoritative text, however, is a book called *The Wealth of Michelangelo* by Rab Hatfield, which took me months to find but was worth it. Hatfield's work covers all the artist's investments, including detailed ledgers and what made Michelangelo the wealthiest artist of the Renaissance. Quotes from Rab Hatfield (who was also hard to track down) come from a phone interview I did with him and subsequent e-mail conversations. The story of Henri Murger comes from Encyclopedia Britannica. The William Wallace quotes are from a personal phone interview and e-mail conversations. References to the New Renaissance are from original research I did for this book, which includes more than two hundred interviews with working creatives.

Sources:

Bruni, Frank. "Florence Journal; The Warts on Michelangelo: The Man Was a Miser." *New York Times*, January 21, 2003. Accessed November 3, 2016. www.nytimes.com/2003/01/21/world/florence-journal-the-warts-on -michelangelo-the-man-was-a-miser.html.

Hatfield, Rab. *The Wealth of Michelangelo*. Rome: Edizioni Di Storia E Letteratura, 2002.

———. Personal phone interview with the author. Florence, Italy. Skype call. February 25, 2016.

Johnstone, Bruce, "Michelangelo Is Branded a Multi-Millionaire Miser." *Telegraph*, November 30, 2002. Accessed November 3, 2016. http://www .telegraph.co.uk/news/worldnews/europe/italy/1414836/Michelangelo-is -branded-a-multi-millionaire-miser.html.

"Henri Murger." Encyclopedia Britannica, last modified August 14, 2007. Accessed November 3, 2016. www.britannica.com/biography/Henri -Murger.

Wallace, William E. *Michelangelo: The Artist, the Man, and His Times*. New York: Cambridge University Press, 2011.

———. Personal phone interview with the author. St. Louis, Missouri. Telephone call. March 28, 2016.

CHAPTER 1

The story of Adrian Cardenas first appeared in an article in the *New Yorker* titled "Why I Quit Major League Baseball." After reading several stories from Cardenas, including the CNN piece about his father's escape from Cuba, I interviewed him over the phone. All original quotes come from that interview. References to Paul Torrance and his work come from a story NPR did on the Torrance Test, as well as personal interviews with Sarah Sumners and Bonnie Cramond, who worked with Professor Torrance and the Torrance Center. *Why Fly?* is also a great primer on his approach to creativity and education. Many of the Michelangelo stories in this book, including the one in this chapter, come from William (Bill) Wallace's biography. The "Should I Quit My Day Job?" study comes from an academic business journal. Gordon Mackenzie's story comes from his book *Orbiting the Giant Hairball*, which is a must-read for any creative. John Grisham's story is from a *USA Today* article by Dennis Moore and a PBS interview Grisham did with Bill Moyers. The Hemingway quote is from a book called *The Wild Years*, which includes previously unpublished letters and essays from the author.

Sources:

Blair, Elizabeth. "More than 50 Years of Putting Kids' Creativity to the Test." NPR.org, April 17, 2013. Accessed November 3, 2016. www.npr.org /2013/04/17/177040995/more-than-50-years-of-putting-kids-creativity -to-the-test.

Cardenas, Adrian. "The U.S. and Cuba: A Love Story." CNN.com, June 4, 2014. Accessed November 3, 2015. http://edition.cnn.com/2015/06/04 /opinions/crdenas-cuba-escape-and-reunion/.

———. "Why I Quit Major League Baseball." *New Yorker*, October 30, 2013. Accessed November 3, 2016. www.newyorker.com/news/sporting-scene /why-i-quit-major-league-baseball.

———. Personal interview with the author. New York, New York. Telephone call. April 28, 2016.

Cramond, Bonnie. Personal interview with the author. Athens, Georgia. Telephone call. April 20, 2016.

Grisham, John. Interview with Bill Moyers. *Bill Moyers Journal*. PBS,
    January 25, 2008. Accessed November 3, 2016. www.pbs.org/moyers
    /journal/archives/grishamexcl_flash.html.

Hemingway, Ernest. *The Wild Years*. New York: Dell, 1967.

MacKenzie, Gordon. *Orbiting the Giant Hairball*. New York: Viking, 1998.

Moore, Dennis. "John Grisham Marks 20th Anniversary of 'A Time to Kill.'" *USA
    Today*, June 22, 2009. Accessed November 3, 2016. http://usatoday30.usatoday.
    com/life/books/news/2009–06–21-john-grisham-a-time-to-kill_N.htm.

Raffiee Joseph and Jie Feng. "Should I Quit My Day Job? A Hybrid Path to
    Entrepreneurship." *Academy of Management Journal* 57, August 1, 2014,
    pp. 936–63. Accessed March 27, 2016. doi:10.5465/amj.2012.0522.

Sumners, Sarah. Personal interview with the author. Athens, Georgia.
    Telephone call. April 20, 2016.

Torrance, Paul E. *Why Fly?* Santa Barbara, CA: Praeger, 1995.

Wallace, William E. *Michelangelo: The Artist, the Man, and His Times*. New York:
    Cambridge University Press, 2011.

CHAPTER 2

Most of the Jim Henson stories come from Brian Jay Jones's biography, which I highly recommend. Additional sources include YouTube videos for *Sam & Friends* and Wilkins commercials. Elizabeth Hyde Stevens's book *Make Art Make Money* also provided some context for how Henson's art drove his business. All references to Mihaly Csikszentmihalyi come from his book *Creativity*. For references to "stealing" during the Renaissance, Noah Charney's work on the subject is revealing. The story of the Irish monk Columcille comes from *The Story of the Irish Race* by Seumas McManus, a great introduction to Irish history. Twyla Tharp's story and quotes come from her book *The Creative Habit* as well as her autobiography *Push Comes to Shove*. The Hunter S. Thompson quotes and story come from *The New Yorker* and *The Paris Review*. For more on creativity as theft, Austin Kleon has some great things to say in *Steal Like an Artist*.

Sources:

Caine, Michael. *Acting in Film*. New York: Applause Theatre and Cinema Books, 1997, 2000.

Charney, Noah. *The Art of Forgery: The Minds, Motives, and Methods of the Master Forgers*. London: Phaidon Press, 2015.

Csikszentmihalyi, Mihaly. *Creativity: The Psychology of Discovery and Invention*. New York: HarperCollins Publishers Ltd., 2013.

Durant, Will. *Heroes of History*. New York: Scribner, 2009.

"Jim Henson's Wilkins Coffee Commercials." YouTube video. Posted July 27, 2010, by Pikachu4352. Accessed March 20, 2016. www.youtube.com /watch?v=ZxLyuw5bdyk.

Jones, Brian Jay. *Jim Henson: The Biography*. New York: Ballantine Books, 2013.

Kleon, Austin. *Steal Like an Artist: 10 Things Nobody Told You About Being Creative*. New York: Workman Publishing Company, 2012.

Louis, Menaud. "Believer." *New Yorker*. March 7, 2005. http://www.newyorker .com/magazine/2005/03/07 believer.

McManus, Seumas. *The Story of the Irish Rose*. New York: Bibliographic Center for Research, 2009.

Menand, Louis. "Believer." *New Yorker*, March 7, 2005. Accessed November 3, 2016. www.newyorker.com/magazine/2005/03/07/believer.

Stevens, Elizabeth Hyde. *Make Art Make Money: Lessons from Jim Henson on Fueling Your Creative Career*. Seattle: Lake Union Publishing, 2014.

Tharp, Twyla. *Push Comes to Shove*. New York: Bantam, 1993.

Tharp, Twyla and Mark Reiter. *The Creative Habit: Learn It and Use It for Life*. New York: Simon & Schuster, 2006.

Thompson, Hunter S. "Hunter S. Thompson, The Art of Journalism No. 1." *Paris Review*. Issue 156, Fall 2000. Interviewed by Douglas Brinkley, Terry McDonell. www.theparisreview.org/interviews/619/hunter-s-thopson-the -art-of-journalism-no-1-hunter-s-thompson.

CHAPTER 3

I first heard about Tia Link from a friend who had read about her career transition in an online interview. I tracked her down and called her while she was in between auditions. I interviewed her over the phone and followed up with some more questions via e-mail. References to apprenticeship and how Michelangelo began to work with Ghirlandaio come from Vasari's work and *Michelangelo: Sculptor and Painter* by Barbara Somervill. Irving Stone's novelized biography of Michelangelo, *The Agony and the Ecstasy*, portrays the dramatic encounter the two men had, but there is some debate among scholars if this happened. What cannot be disputed, however, is that there was some money exchanged between the men during Michelangelo's brief apprenticeship. Whatever the arrangement, it was an unusual one. Wallace's biography shares more on why that might be, arguing that the Buonarroti family, though technically not nobility, had some connection to the Medici, which probably allowed Michelangelo to secure opportunities that weren't available to others.

Sources:

Link, Tia. Personal interview with the author. New York, NY, March 9, 2016.

Somervill, Barbara A. *Michelangelo: Sculptor and Painter*. Minneapolis: Compass Point Books, 2005.

Stone, Irving. *The Agony and the Ecstasy: A Biographical Novel of Michelangelo*. London: Arrow Books, 1997.

Vasari, Giorgio. *The Lives of the Artists*. Translated by Julia Conway Bondanella and Peter Bondanella. Oxford: Oxford Paperbacks, 2008.

Wallace, William E. *Michelangelo: The Artist, the Man, and His Times*. Cambridge: Cambridge University Press, 2011.

CHAPTER 4

The story of F. Scott Fitzgerald comes from several different sources. The one I enjoyed the most was a biography about his book *The Great Gatsby* called *So We Read On*, by Maureen Corrigan. Other sources are included below. Zach Prichard's story about fundraising for Donald Miller was told to me personally over a series of interviews in person and by phone. The Michelangelo story in this chapter comes from Condivi. Angela Duckworth's work on grit can be found by reading her book or groundbreaking research paper of the same title. She also has an excellent TED talk on the subject. The Jeff Bezos and Amazon stories came from a series of articles online and *The Everything Store*. The Steve Jobs conversation is from an article you can find online, but his "reality distortion field" was an important subject in Walter Isaacson's biography on Jobs as well.

Sources:

Blue Origin. https://www.blueorigin.com/.

Bulygo, Zack. "12 Business Lessons You Can Learn from Amazon Founder and CEO Jeff Bezos." KISSMetrics, January 19, 2013. Accessed November 3, 2016. https://blog.kissmetrics.com/lessons-from-jeff-bezos/.

Condivi, Ascanio. *The Life of Michelangelo.* Baton Rouge: Louisiana State University Press, 1975.

Corrigan, Maureen. *So We Read On: How* The Great Gatsby *Came to Be and Why It Endures.* New York: Little, Brown and Company, 2014.

Duckworth, Angela L., Christopher Peterson, Michael D. Matthews and Dennis R. Kelly. "Grit: Perseverance and Passion for Long-Term Goals." *Journal of Personality and Social Psychology* 92, no. 6 (2007): 1087–1101. Accessed online through the School of Arts and Sciences at the University of Pennsylvania, November 3, 2016. www.sas.upenn.edu/~duckwort/images /Grit%20JPSP.pdf.

Duckworth, Angela L. "Grit: The Power of Passion and Perseverance." TED Talks Education, 6:12, April 2013. Accessed November 3, 2016. www.ted .com/talks/angela_lee_duckworth_grit_the_power_of_passion_and _perseverance?language=en.

Fitzgerald, F. Scott; Matthew J. Bruccoli compiler. *A Life in Letters: F. Scott Fitzgerald.* New York: Scribner, 1995.

Fundable. "Amazon Startup Story." Fundable.com. Accessed November 3, 2016. www.fundable.com/learn/startup-stories/amazon.

Greathouse, John. "5 Time-Tested Success Tips from Amazon Founder Jeff Bezos." *Forbes*, April 30, 2013. Accessed November 3, 2016. www.forbes.com/sites/johngreathouse/2013/04/30/5-time-tested-success-tips-from-amazon-founder-jeff-bezos/#67f1b6c63351.

Hertzfeld, Andy. "Reality Distortion Field." Folklore.com. Accessed November 3, 2016. www.folklore.org/StoryView.py?story=Reality_Distortion_Field.txt.

Isaacson, Walter. *Steve Jobs*. New York: Simon and Schuster, 2011, 2013.

Kantor, David and David Streitfeld. "Inside Amazon: Wrestling Big Ideas in a Bruising Workplace." *New York Times*, August 15, 2015. Accessed November 3, 2016. www.nytimes.com/2015/08/16/technology/inside-amazon-wrestling-big-ideas-in-a-bruising-workplace.html.

Lerman, Rachel. "Amazon's Headcount Tops 150,000 After Adding Nearly 40,000 Employees in 2014." *Puget Sound Business Journal*, January 29, 2015. Accessed November 3, 2016. www.bizjournals.com/seattle/blog/techflash/2015/01/amazons-headcount-tops-150–000-after-adding.html.

Mental Floss. "How WWII Saved 'The Great Gatsby' from Obscurity." *Mental Floss*, April 6, 2015. Accessed November 3, 2016. http://mentalfloss.com/article/62358/how-wwii-saved-great-gatsby-obscurity.

Prichard, Zach. Personal interview with the author. Skype call. Franklin, TN, September 14, 2016.

Quirk, William J. "Living on $500,000 a Year." *American Scholar*, September 1, 2009. Accessed November 3, 2016. https://theamericanscholar.org/living-on-500000-a-year/#.WBuSJOErKRs.

Scheidies, Nick. "15 Business Lessons from Amazon's Jeff Bezos." *Income*. Accessed November 3, 2016. www.incomediary.com/15-business-lessons-from-amazons-jeff-bezos.

Statista. "Net sales revenue of Amazon from 2004 to 2016." Statista.com. Accessed November 3, 2016. www.statista.com/statistics/266282/annual-net-revenue-of-amazoncom/.

Szalavitz, Maia. "Creativity Linked with Deficit in Mental Flexibility." *Time*, June 7, 2013. Accessed November 3, 2016. http://healthland.time.com/2013/06/07/creativity-linked-with-deficit-in-mental-flexibility/.

Trevor, Will. "Amazon & Leadership: The 14 Leadership Principles (Part 1)." LinkedIn, November 11, 2014. Accessed November 3, 2016. www.linkedin.com/pulse/20141111222354–23565607-amazon-s-14-leadership-principles-part-1.

Wallace, William E. *Michelangelo: The Artist, the Man, and His Times.* New York: Cambridge University Press, 2011.

Chapter 5

The story of how Elvis met Sam Phillips is recounted in two books by Peter Guralnick: *Last Train to Memphis*, which is told from Elvis's perspective, and *Sam Phillips*, which is from Phillips's perspective. You can also find this story online in a few articles and interviews. References to Elizabeth Currid-Halkett's work on tastemakers and the creative economy comes from her book *The Warhol Economy* and a phone interview I did with her. The Michelangelo story comes from the Forcellino biography. Kabir Sehgal's story came from an article and interview I did with him just before he was deployed overseas. References to Michael Hyatt come from in-person conversations and e-mail correspondence.

Sources:

Cash, Johnny, Patrick Carr, *Cash: The Autobiography* (New York: HarperCollins, 1997), 101–111.

Currid-Halkett, Elizabeth. Personal interview with the author. Skype call. Los Angeles, CA, March 8, 2016.

———. *The Warhol Economy: How Fashion, Art, and Music Drive.* New York: Princeton University Press, 2008.

Forcellino, Antonio. *Michelangelo: A Tormented Life.* Cambridge: Polity, 2011.

Guralnick, Peter. "Elvis Presley: How Sun Records boss Sam Phillips discovered a star in 1954." *Independent*, October 30, 2013. Accessed November 3, 2016. www.independent.co.uk/arts-entertainment/music/features/elvis-presley-how-sun-records-boss-sam-phillips-discovered-a-star-in-1954-a6713891.html.

———. *Last Train to Memphis: The Rise of Elvis Presley.* New York: Back Bay Books, 1995.

———. *Sam Phillips: The Man Who Invented Rock 'n' Roll.* New York: Little, Brown and Company, 2015.

Hyatt, Michael. Personal interview with the author. E-mail. Franklin, TN, August 12, 2016.

Sehgal, Kabir. "How I made it from Wall Street to the Grammys." CNBC, April 26, 2016. Accessed November 3, 2016. www.cnbc.com/2016/04/26 /how-i-made-it-from-wall-street-to-the-grammys-commentary.html.

———. Personal interview with the author. Skype call. Atlanta, GA, May 2, 2016.

CHAPTER 6

Hemingway's story of moving to Paris is told in its entirety in the book *Hemingway: The Paris Years* by Michael Reynolds, which is part of a five-part series on the author. It is well worth reading. Richard Florida's work on the creative class is covered in his book *The Rise of the Creative Class* and an interview I did with him. The Patti Smith quote comes from an interview she did. Her book *Just Kids* is a wonderful insight into the scene that was 1970s New York. Eric Weiner's book *Geography of Genius* is a funny, thoughtful, and entertaining read for anyone curious about creative clusters and the reasons behind them. Hank Willis Thomas's story comes from a phone interview. I used a few references from online articles and his website to fill in the gaps. The Van Gogh story comes from a few sources; the most interesting to read is Irving Stone's novelized biography of him, which, apparently, is meticulous in its research. For a better picture of how the Impressionists created their own network, read Ross King's *The Judgment of Paris*. I found Tracy Weisel through a friend who happened to be visiting the town of Jerome, Arizona, and told me I had to hear his story. The Brontë sisters' story comes from Catherine Reef's biography.

Sources:

Csikszentmihalyi, Mihaly. *Creativity: The Psychology of Discovery and Invention.* New York: HarperCollins Publishers Ltd., 2013.

Florida, Richard. Personal interview with the author. Skype call. March 14, 2016.

——. *The Rise of the Creative Class.* New York: Basic Books, 2003.

Hank Willis Thomas (website). Accessed November 3, 2016. www .hankwillisthomas.com.

Jack Shainman Gallery. "Hank Willis Thomas." Jackshainman.com. Accessed November 3, 2016. www.jackshainman.com/artists/hankwillis-thomas/.

King, Ross. *The Judgment of Paris: The Revolutionary Decade That Gave the World Impressionism.* New York: Walker & Company, 2006.

Reef, Catherine. *The Brontë Sisters: The Brief Lives of Charlotte, Emily, and Anne.* New York: Clarion Books, 2015.

Reynolds, Michael. *Hemingway: The Paris Years.* New York: WW Norton, 1995.

Rodulfo, Kristina. "Patti Smith: New York Is No Longer Welcoming to Artists and Dreamers." *Elle*, October 6, 2015. Accessed November 3, 2016. http:// www.elle.com/culture/books/news/a31004/new-york-city-then-and-now -according-to-patti-smith/.

Smith, Patti. *M. Train.* New York: Vintage Books, 2015, 2016.

Stone, Irving. *Lust for Life.* New York: Plume, 1984.

The Royal Academy (website). Accessed November 3, 2016. https://www .royalacademy.org.uk/.

Thomas, Hank Willis. Personal interview with the author. New York, NY. March 21, 2016.

Van Gogh Museum. "How many paintings did Van Gogh sell in his lifetime?" Van Gogh Museum. Accessed November 3, 2016. https://www.vangoghmuseum .nl/en/125-questions/questions-and-answers/question-54-of-125.

Weiner, Eric. Personal interview with the author. Skype call. June 15, 2016.

——. *The Geography of Genius: A Search for the World's Most Creative Places from Ancient Athens to Silicon Valley.* New York: Simon & Schuster, 2016.

Weisel, Tracy. Personal interview with the author. Telephone call. Jerome, AZ, May 5, 2016.

CHAPTER 7

Diana Glyer's research on the Inklings is compelling, and the interview I did with her was no less inspiring than her books *The Company They Keep* and *Bandersnatch*. For more on collaborative circles, read

Michael Farrell's work on the subject. I also interviewed Keith Sawyer whose book *Group Genius* is an easy but informative read on the communal nature of creativity. Gary Monroe's retelling of the story of the Highwaymen is fascinating; all his books on the subject are well worth reading. I interviewed Caroline Robinson about her experience of starting her business and what she learned. References to Michelangelo being an entrepreneur and manager come from William Wallace's book *Michelangelo at San Lorenzo* and our interview.

Sources:

Clear Mapping Company (website). Accessed November 3, 2016. www.clearmapping
.co.uk/about-us.html.

Farrell, Michael. *Collaborative Circles: Friendship Dynamics and Creative Work.*
Chicago: University of Chicago Press, 2003.

Glyer, Diana. Personal interview with the author. Skype call. Azusa, CA,
April 1, 2016.

———. *Bandersnatch: C. S. Lewis, J. R. R. Tolkien and the Creative Collaboration
of the Inklings.* Kent, OH: Kent Univ. Press, 2015.

Jones, Jonathan. "And the Winner Is . . . How a Bitter Painting Contest
Between Michelangelo and Leonardo Became One of the Most
Extraordinary Episodes of the Renaissance." *Guardian*, October 22, 2002.
Accessed November 3, 2016. www.theguardian.com/culture/2002/oct/22
/artsfeatures.highereducation.

McKinney, Kelsey. "Beyoncé's 'Lemonade': How the Writing Credits Reveal
Her Genius." *Fusion*, April 25, 2016. Accessed November 3, 2016. http://
fusion.net/story/294943/beyonce-lemonade-writers/.

Monroe, Gary. Personal interview with the author. Skype call. March 24, 2016.

———. *The Highwaymen: Florida's African-American Landscape Painters.*
Gainesville: University Press of Florida, 2001.

Robinson, Caroline. Personal interview with the author. Skype call. May 5,
2016.

Sawyer, Keith. *Group Genius: The Creative Power of Collaboration.* New York:
Basic Books, 2008.

———. Personal interview with the author. Skype call. February 4, 2016.

Wallace, William E. *Michelangelo at San Lorenzo: The Genius as Entrepreneur.*
    Cambridge: Cambridge University Press, 1994.
    ———. *Michelangelo: The Artist, the Man, and His Times.* Cambridge: Cambridge
    University Press, 2011.
    ———. Personal interview with the author. St. Louis, MO, March 28, 2016.

CHAPTER 8

Stephanie Halligan's story comes from a personal interview I did with
her. You can learn more about her at her blog *Art to Self.* The story of
Picasso comes from the book *In Montmartre* by Sue Roe as well as an
article in *Forbes* on the artist's business savviness. The Chris Rock
story comes from an article by Peter Sims. Led Zeppelin's story of
launching a record without their name is recounted on the Superhype
Blog, where I first found it, but you can also read about it in Jimmy
Page's own words in the book *Light and Shade.*

Sources:

Adamson, Allen. "What Picasso Knew: Branding Tips for Artists from an Art
    Basel Insider." *Forbes*, May 22, 2013. Accessed November 3, 2016. www
    .forbes.com/sites/allenadamson/2013/05/22/what-picasso-knew-branding
    -tips-for-artists-from-an-art-basel-insider/#690466a62b64.
Build Network Staff. "The Marketing Genius of Led Zeppelin IV." *Inc.*,
    June 20, 2013. Accessed November 3, 2016. www.inc.com/thebuildnetwork
    /the-marketing-genius-of-led-zeppelin-iv.html.
Case, George. *Led Zeppelin FAQ: All That's Left to Know About the Greatest Hard
    Rock Band of All Time.* London: Backbeat Books, 2011.
Deal, David. "The Marketing Genius of Led Zeppelin IV." Superhype Blog,
    April 29, 2011. Accessed November 3, 2016. http://superhypeblog.com
    /marketing/the-marketing-genius-of-led-zeppelin-iv.
Halligan, Stephanie. "Let Yourself Be Seen" (Cartoon). Art to Self. Accessed
    November 3, 2016. www.arttoself.com/2016/07/14/let-yourself-be-seen/.
    ———. Personal interview with the author. Skype call. Boulder, CO, April 14, 2016.

Kleon, Austin. *Show Your Work!* New York: Workman Publishing Co., 2014.

Roe, Sue. *In Montmartre: Picasso, Matisse, and the Birth of Modernist Art.* New York: Penguin Press, 2015.

Sand, George. *Letters of George Sand*, Vol. 3. London: Forgotten Books, 2012.

Sims, Peter. "Think Like Chris Rock: Little Bets." Peter Sims Blog, July 15, 2010. Accessed November 3, 2016. http://petersims.com/2010/07/15/think-chrisrock/.

Tolinski, Brad. *Light and Shade: Conversations with Jimmy Page.* Toronto: McClelland & Stewart, 2013.

CHAPTER 9

Melissa Dinwiddie told me her story over Skype and via e-mail correspondence. The article by Jordan Weissmann in the *Atlantic* talks about why unpaid internships don't lead to paid gigs. The Michelangelo stories come from Amy Helms and Miles Unger. Harlan Ellison's rant on why you should pay the writer is a wonderfully profane rant on why creative workers deserve their wages; you can find it on YouTube. Bill Ivey's take on commercial art comes from an interview I did with him, but you can learn a lot from his book *Arts, Inc.* Paul Jarvis quotes come from a conversation I had with him for my podcast, *The Portfolio Life*, which you can listen to online.

Sources:

Dinwiddie, Melissa. Personal interview with the author. Skype call. July 15, 2015.

Helms, Amy. "Michelangelo and the High Renaissance." *Prezi*, September 17, 2015. Accessed November 3, 2016. https://prezi.com/ekerk1rmduok /michelangelo-and-the-high-renaissance/.

Horton, Nicholas. "Harlan Ellison—Pay the Writer." YouTube, posted November 7, 2007. Accessed November 3, 2016. www.youtube.com /watch?v=mj5IV23g-fE.

Ivey, Bill. *Arts, Inc.: How Greed and Neglect Have Destroyed Our Cultural Rights.* Berkeley, CA: University of California Press, 2008.

———. Personal interview with the author. Nashville, TN, April 7, 2016.

Jarvis, Paul. Personal interview with the author. Skype call. January 7, 2017.

Marshall, Colin. "Harlan Ellison's Wonderful Rant on Why Writers Should Always Get Paid." *Open Culture*, November 6, 2015. Accessed November 3, 2016. www.openculture.com/2015/11/harlan-ellisons-wonderful-rant-on -why-writers-should-always-get-paid.html.

Unger, Miles J. *Michelangelo: A Life in Six Masterpieces*. New York: Simon & Schuster, 2014.

Weissmann, Jordan. "Do Unpaid Internships Lead to Jobs? Not for College Students." *Atlantic*, June 19, 2013. Accessed November 3, 2016. www .theatlantic.com/business/archive/2013/06/do-unpaid-internships-lead-to -jobs-not-for-college-students/276959/.

CHAPTER 10

The Shakespeare story comes from a biography by James Shapiro called *1599*, in which he tells the story of one year in the Bard's life and why it was so impactful. How Jay-Z eventually owned his masters is told in Zack O'Malley Greenburg's book *Empire State of Mind*. The story of Pixar is told in Glenn Beck's book *Dreamers and Deceivers*. Stephen Kellogg's story comes from an interview I did with him. You can find his solo work online and support his most recent record, which I am enjoying. The story of how George Lucas maintained a majority ownership in *Star Wars* is told in Chris Taylor's wonderful book *How Star Wars Conquered the Universe*. (As a Star Wars geek, I was a fan.) I first read the Cirque du Soleil story in Lewis Schiff's book *Business Brilliant* and eventually read more about it online. The Prince quote comes from an article.

Sources:

Beck, Glenn. *Dreamers and Deceivers: True Stories of the Heroes and Villains Who Made America*. New York: Threshold Editions, 2014.

Brown, August. "What Today's Artists Learn from Prince's Approach to the Industry." *LA Times*, April 22, 2016. Accessed November 3, 2016. www .latimes.com.entertainment/music/posts/la-et-ms-prince-imaginative-legacy -music-business-20160422-story.html.

Greenburg, Zack O'Malley. *Empire State of Mind: How Jay-Z Went from Street Corner to Corner Office*. New York: Portfolio, 2015.

Gupta, Vivek and Manasi Pawar. "Cirque du Soleil HRM Practices." IBS Center for Management Research, 2007. www.icmrindia.org/case.studios /catalogue/.

Kellogg, Stephen. Personal interview with the author. Telephone call. March 28, 2016.

Pollock, Dale. *Skywalking: The Life and Films of George Lucas, updated edition*. Boston: DaCapo Press, 1999.

Schiff, Lewis. *Business Brilliant*. New York: HarperCollins, 2013.

Shapiro, James. *A Year in the Life of William Shakespeare: 1599*. New York: Harper Perennial, 2006.

Stephen Kellogg (website). Accessed November 3, 2016. www.stephenkellogg.com/.

Taylor, Chris. *How Star Wars Conquered the Universe: The Past, Present, and Future of a Multibillion Dollar Franchise*. New York: Basic Books, 2014.

Chapter 11

Mark Frauenfelder's story comes from an interview I did with him, but you can read more about him online by searching his name. Chuck Chapman shared with me over the phone his experiences of dealing with ADHD as a therapist and why he thinks it drives creative output. You can also read more on this subject by Scott Barry Kaufman and Darya Zabelina, whom I also interviewed. The Michael Jackson story comes from a *Forbes* article. The bit on artist revenue streams comes from a paper that was published by Kristin Thomson and Jean Cook. Charles Handy's work on portfolios comes from *The Age of Unreason* and has influenced a lot of my work and how I perceive it. I even named my podcast *The Portfolio Life* after his philosophy on the future of work.

Sources:

Boing Boing (website). Accessed November 3, 2016. http://boingboing.net/about.

Chapman, Chuck. Personal interview with the author. Skype call. April 19, 2016.

Frauenfelder, Mark. Personal interview with the author. Skype call. February 3, 2016.

Greenburg, Zack O'Malley. "Michael Jackson: Secret Business Genius?" *Forbes*, January 25, 2011. Accessed November 3, 2016. www.forbes.com/sites /zackomalleygreenburg/2011/01/25/michael-jackson-secret-business-genius -music-business/#2265f37198e4.

Handy, Charles. *The Age of Unreason*. Cambridge, MA: Harvard Business School Press, 1990.

Kaufman, Scott Barry. "The Creative Gifts of ADHD." *Scientific American*, October 21, 2014. Accessed November 3, 2016. https://blogs.scientificamerican .com/beautiful-minds/the-creative-gifts-of-adhd/.

Mark Frauenfelder (website). Accessed November 3, 2016. www.markfrauenfelder .com/.

Thomson, Kristin and Jean Cook. "Artist Revenue Streams: A Multi-Method Research Project Examining Changes in Musicians' Sources of Income." Accessed from the Berkman Klein Center for Internet and Society at Harvard University, November 3, 2016. https://cyber.law.harvard.edu/sites/cyber.law .harvard.edu/files/Rethinking_Music_Artist_Revenue_Streams.pdf.

Zabelina, Darya. Personal interview with the author. Skype call. Chicago, IL. May 2, 2016.

CHAPTER 12

The story of *kamishibai* is covered in various articles and books, which are listed below. Alan Bean's incredible experience of becoming the first astronaut artist is covered in numerous books, including *Apollo*. I spoke with Alan on the phone and was captivated by his story and approach to creative work. You can learn more about him by accessing his website where you can view his vast body of work, including a piece currently available for over $400,000 if you want to buy a painting with some moon dust. Lewis Hyde's research on how art is a gift is covered in *The Gift*. I also interviewed him. The Walt Disney quote comes from a book called *Walt: Backstage Adventures with Walt Disney*.

Sources:

Alan Bean (website). Accessed November 3, 2016. www.alanbean.com/.

Bean, Alan. *Apollo: An Eyewitness Account by Artist/Astronaut/Moonwalker Alan Bean*. Seymour, CT: The Greenwich Workshop Press, 1998.

——. Personal interview with the author. Skype call. Houston, TX, April 8, 2016.

Hyde, Lewis. Personal interview with the author. Phone call. May 11, 2016.

McCarthy, Helen. *A Brief History of Manga*. London: Ilex Press. July 15, 2014.

——. *The Gift: Creativity and the Artist in the Modern World*. New York: Vintage Books, 2007.

McGowan, Tara. "Kamishibai: A Brief History." Kamishibai.com. Accessed November 3, 2016. www.kamishibai.com/history.html.

Shows, Charles. *Walt: Backstage Adventures with Walt Disney*. Los Angeles: Communications Creativity, 1979.

Yusuke, Kubo. "Kyoto 'Paper Drama' master Yassan." *Kyoto Journal*. Accessed November 3, 2016. www.kyotojournal.org/renewal/kyoto-kamishibai-master/.

CONCLUSION

I first heard the "Modigliani's heads" story from Rab Hatfield as an example of how people will believe what they want to believe, even if it's not true. This was during the same conversation in which he told me about how he found Michelangelo's wealth. I tracked down the rest of the story through online articles and interviews.

Sources:

Art Is Life. "Fake Modigliani heads get a museum of their own," Art is Life Blog. Accessed May 15, 2016, https://artislimited.wordpress.com/2013/10/12/fake-modigliani-heads-get-a-museum-of-their-own-thirty-years-after-the-controversial-hoax/.

Livorno Now (website). "Modigliani's heads," Livorno Now. Accessed November 3, 2016. www.livornonow.com/modiglianis_heads.

Natanson, Ann. "Three Students and a Dockworker Put Their Heads Together and Confound the Art World." *People*, October 8, 1984. Accessed November 3, 2016. http://people.com/archive/three-students-and-a-dockworker -put-their-heads-together-and-confound-the-art-world-vol-22-no-15/.

Phillips, John. "Modigliani Head May Be Work of Pranksters." *UPI*, September 11, 1984. Accessed November 3, 2016. www.upi.com/Archives/1984/09/11 /Modigliani-head-may-be-work-of-pranksters/3010463723200/.

About the Author

JEFF GOINS IS A BESTSELLING AUTHOR, KEYNOTE SPEAKER, AND popular blogger with a reputation for challenging the status quo. In three years, Goins built a million-dollar business, published four books, and became an online marketing expert, using his skills in writing and business to help others succeed. He is the author of four books, including *The Art of Work*, which landed on the bestseller lists of *USA Today*, *Publisher's Weekly*, and *Washington Post*. He lives with his family near Nashville, Tennessee. Visit him online at goinswriter.com.